THE CONWY VA
WAY

A long-distance walk around the beautiful Conwy Valley from Conwy Bay to the river's source at Llyn Conwy, linking Llandudno, Llanrwst, Betws-y-Coed, Conwy and other historic communities

David Berry

KITTIWAKE

About the author

David is an experienced walker, with an interest in local history. He is the author of a many Kittiwake walks guidebooks covering North Wales, where he lives. Whether on a riverside ramble or mountain walk he greatly appreciates the beauty, culture and history of the landscape and hopes that his comprehensive guidebooks will encourage people to explore on foot its diverse scenery and rich heritage.

He has undertaken many long distance walks, including coast-to-coast crossings of England, Scotland and Wales. He has used this experience to devise The Dee Way, a long distance cross border walk following the river Dee to its source in Southern Snowdonia.

He has worked as a Rights of Way surveyor across North Wales, been a freelance writer for Walking Wales magazine, and has served as a member of Denbighshire Local Access Forum.

For more information visit www.davidberrywalks.co.uk

Thanks

I wish to thank John Lamprell, who had enjoyed walking my Dee Way, for suggesting the idea of a similar trail for the river Conwy. Also thanks to the National Trust's Ysbyty Estate Warden, Welsh Water Authority and Conwy Borough Council's Rights of Way Section.

David Berry

Published by Kittiwake
3 Glantwymyn Village Workshops, Glantwymyn, Machynlleth,
Montgomeryshire SY20 8LY

Printed by MWL, Pontypool.

ISBN: 978 1 902302 46 1

Contents

Introduction

The Route

Guidance Notes and Useful Information

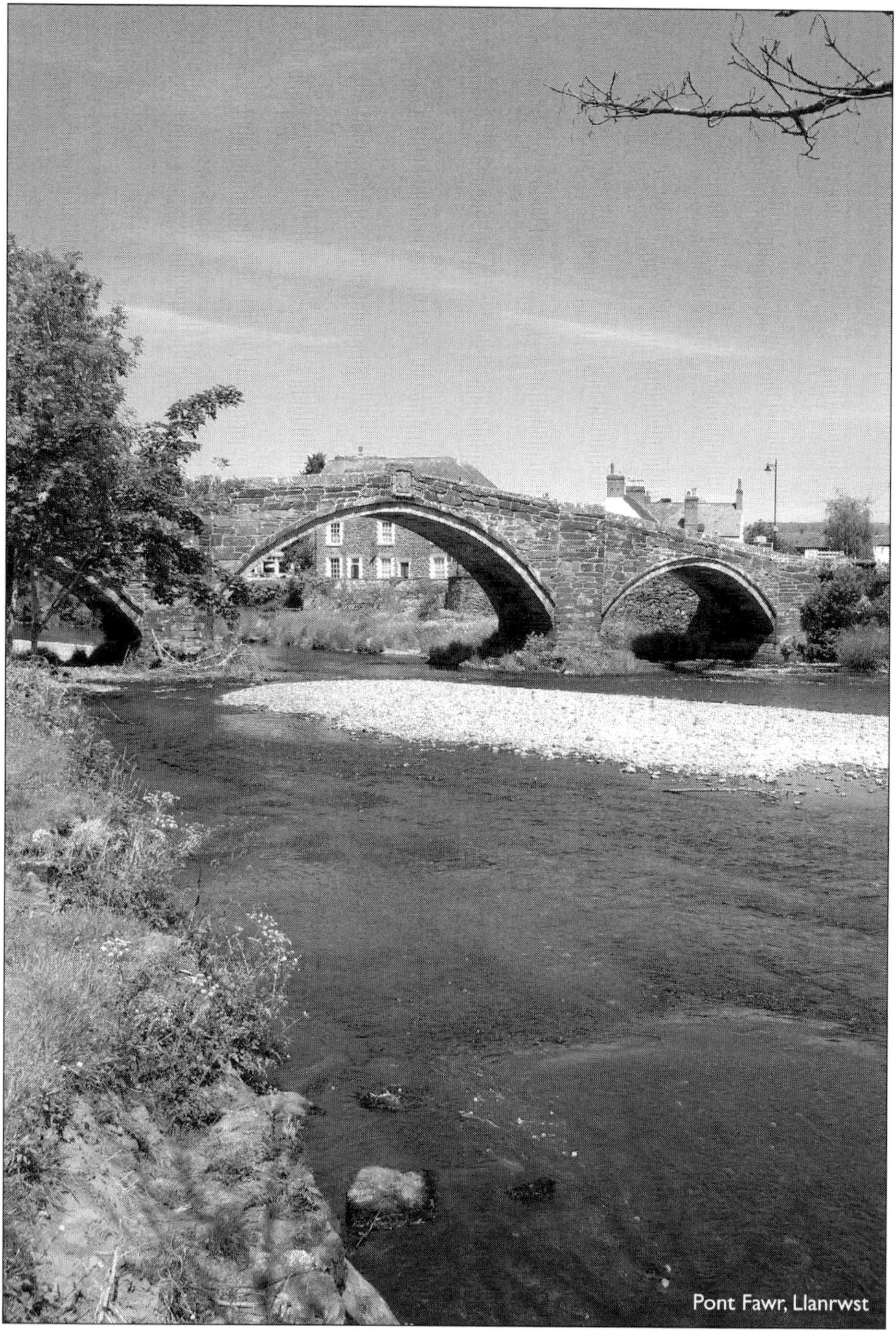

Pont Fawr, Llanrwst

INTRODUCTION

The Conwy Valley

The Afon Conwy is one of the most beautiful rivers in Wales, flowing through a stunning and diverse landscape on the eastern edge of Snowdonia National Park, and passing historic towns and villages. The river rises from Llyn Conwy and tributary streams high amongst the wild desolate moorland of the Migneint – one of the largest in Wales. After a few miles of treeless terrain featuring waterfalls and gorges the river passes through enclosed upland pasture and the small village of Ysbyty Ifan, part of a large estate owned by the National Trust. Later as it tumbles through gorges between wooded hills it is joined by the tributary rivers of the Machno and the Lledr, then by the Llugwy at Betws-y-Coed, the popular inland resort and gateway to Snowdonia.

From Betws-y-Coed the river flows gently north along a widening lush fertile glacial valley grazed by dairy cattle and sheep, passing the historic market town of Llanrwst, the former inland port and spa village of Trefriw, and then the industrial village of Dolgarrog. It continues north to pass between the great medieval walled town of Conwy, a World Heritage Site, and Deganwy to the mouth of the estuary. Here it enters the sea at Conwy Bay, with its sand dunes and beaches, protected on its western side by the impressive limestone headland of the Great Orme.

Over its journey from source to sea this majestic river descends nearly 1500 feet. It is tidal as far as Llanrwst during spring tides and the lower valley is prone to flooding after heavy rain. The Afon Conwy is one of the finest sea trout rivers in Britain and home to migrating salmon who use a fish pass built in Conwy Falls in the 1990s to gain access to the upper river. The tidal estuary is an important habitat for wading birds such as the curlew and oyster catcher as well as other species. In addition, the Conwy RSPB Nature Reserve, a legacy of the Conwy tunnel excavations, supports a wide range of birds, whilst the cliffs of the Great Orme are home to large numbers of sea birds.

The upland landscape that borders the main valley north from Betws-y-Coed is full of contrasts. On its eastern side it consists of part wooded rolling hills and traditional enclosed upland pasture, through which pass a network of quiet country roads. It boasts one of Britain's most beautiful gardens – Bodnant Gardens – and two classic viewpoints. By contrast the west side of the valley is more rugged in nature, leading to the foothills of the Carneddau mountains. From Betws-y-Coed to Dolgarrog the land rises steeply up wooded slopes, down which rivers flow to join the Afon Conwy. Gwydyr Forest Park, which extends north from Penmachno to Trefriw, forms a large part of this landscape. It occupies an undulating upland plateau divided by the valleys of the Llugwy, Lledr and Machno rivers. The landscape of this part-open forest was shaped by lead and zinc mining, which was at its most active between 1850-1919. This fascinating area at the western edge of the Conwy valley features delightful upland reservoirs, which once provided water for the mines, many relics of this once thriving industry, and good mountain views. Coed Dolgarrog above the village is a designated National Nature Reserve because of its relatively rare woodland.

The higher slopes above Dolgarrog, extending north above Rowen as far as the Conwy Mountain, are particularly rich in evidence of early human settlement in the Conwy valley. Among the many sites of historical interest are standing stones, burial chambers, hut circles, and Iron Age hillforts. The Romans had a presence in the valley, establishing Canovium garrison near the strategic crossing of the Afon Conwy, part of the Roman road from Deva (Chester) to Segontium (Caernarfon) They were also involved in early mining activities and discovered the iron rich spring at Trefriw, which later became famous for its healing properties and remains today as the Trefriw Wells Spa.

For centuries ferry services operated across the river at Deganwy, and also at Tal-y-Cafn, where drovers crossed with their cattle at low tide. The first bridge across the Afon Conwy was Pont Fawr, at Llanrwst, built in 1636. In later years other important and historic bridges were built across the river. At Betws-y-Coed Thomas Telford's bridge (1815), one of the first made from cast iron, carried the London-Holyhead Irish Mail road. At Conwy is Telford's graceful suspension bridge (1826) and the adjacent tubular railway bridge built by Robert Stephenson, which opened in 1849. These bridges were engineering feats of their day. Although not so attractive to the eye, perhaps the same can be said about the more recent Conwy Tunnel (1991), where the tube sections were floated into position in the river.

In earlier centuries the lower valley witnessed periods of warfare and years of struggle between the Welsh and English, when the river's mouth was defended by various castles at Deganwy. Little now remains of this traditional defensive position, but on the other side of the river the formidable Conwy castle still stands, built by Edward I after his successful campaign against Wales.

During the 19thC there were invaders of a different kind when the stunning scenery attracted many eminent travellers, visitors and artists to this part of North Wales. They came by road, by river as far as Trefriw, and later by a railway which was built along the valley from Llandudno Junction to Llanrwst in1863, then extended to Betws-y-Coed in 1868. As well as passenger traffic the line once serviced the slate industry, agriculture and forestry. Nowadays the line remains important for local communities and tourism.

The Conwy Valley Way

The Conwy Valley is a beautiful part of North Wales, steeped in history that attracts thousands of visitors each year. Its diverse landscape of hills, moorland, forest, woodland, upland pasture, wooded valleys, rivers, lakes, estuary and coastal scenery along with its many sites of historical interest, makes it a fascinating area to explore on foot.

The western side of the valley, especially Gwydyr Forest Parc around Betws-y-Coed with its forest trails, is a popular walking area. Less well known is its eastern side, where a paucity of footpaths limits the scope for circular walks, and its more remote upper valley. The best way therefore to fully appreciate the stunning scenery and history of the Conwy Valley is to explore its length from sea to source.

This is my second long distance walking trail after the publication by Kittiwake in 2009 of The Dee Way, which followed the river from the mouth of the estuary to its source in the southern area of Snowdonia National Park. Whilst shorter in length the Conwy Valley Way follows similar principles.

The trail that I have devised offers:

– a continuous long distance trail of up to 102 miles exploring both sides of the Conwy Valley from the mouth of the estuary to its source high on the Migneint moors, with a choice of routes on some sections.

– a route that incorporates the valley's diverse landscape features, classic viewpoints, historic towns and villages, as well as other sites of historical interest.

– a route that links three of North Wales most popular tourist destinations – Llandudno, Betws-y-Coed and Conwy.

– a start (Llandudno) and finish (Conwy) that are linked to the National Rail Network to facilitate easy access from and departure to anywhere in Britain.

– opportunities for multi-day walks and day/half day walks of variable lengths. A key feature of the trail is that it is supported by easily accessible public transport throughout its length, allowing each section to be undertaken as linear day walks. I have broken the trail down into 16 linear walks linked to local transport, which can easily be combined with others to provide longer day walks if necessary.

– a fascinating insight into the history of the valley and the various communities that the trail passes through.

The trail follows public rights of way, permissive paths and crosses Open Access land, using a combination of paths, scenic minor roads, tracks, forest trails, and designated cycle/walkways. It falls within the Conwy County Borough Council area.

This new trail will appeal to people of all ages and abilities. The route will attract experienced walkers who enjoy the challenge of completing a continuous themed walking trail, people who simply seek the tranquility of attractive river, estuary or hill scenery, or those who want to learn more about an area's rich heritage by visiting places of historical interest as part of a walk

Overview of the trail

The Great Orme, protecting the entrance to Conwy Bay and easily accessed from Llandudno with its public transport links, is a natural starting point to this long distance trail. A walk around this impressive limestone headland, with its stunning cliffs and breathtaking views across the bay and the mouth of the Conwy estuary makes a spectacular introduction to the trail. After descending to West Shore promenade it follows the designated Conwy Estuary Trail above the shore to Deganwy and on along the edge of the estuary, with a good view across to Conwy and its castle. After visiting Conwy RSPB Nature Reserve the trail passes through Llandudno Junction, then heads south to begin its journey along the eastern side of the Conwy Valley.

After leaving Glan Conwy it crosses attractive farmland, featuring good

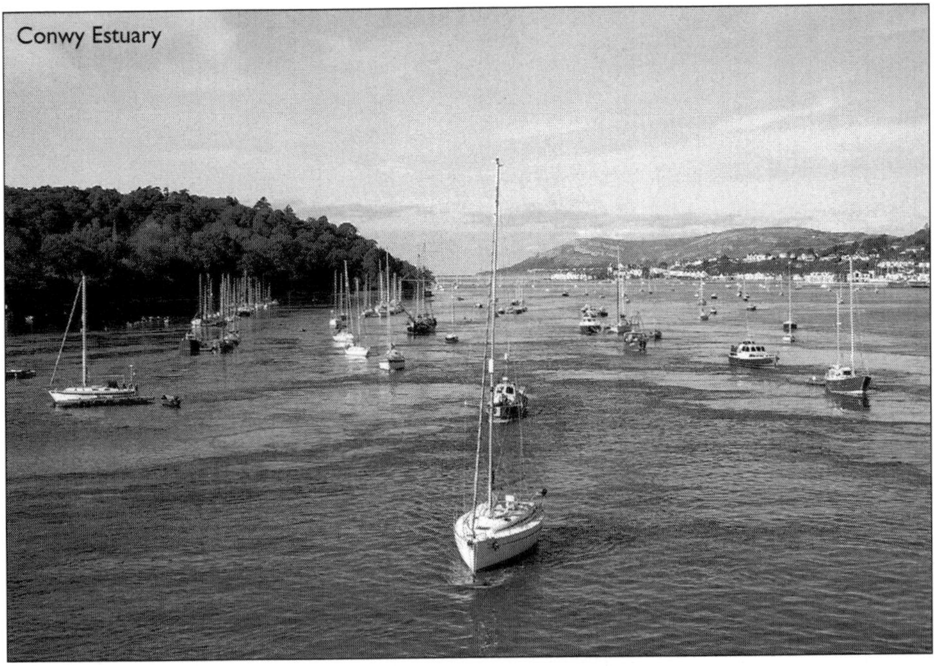

views across the river and an ancient burial chamber, then follows an undulating meandering route to pass near to Bodnant Gardens, one of Britain's most beautiful gardens, which you are encouraged to visit. The next section follows minor scenic country roads across part wooded upland pasture and past a remote lake, then woodland paths to the dramatic Conwy Valley viewpoint of Cadair Ifan Goch crag, owned by the National Trust. Afterwards it descends to the small rural community of Maenan, from where you have an option of following minor upland roads direct to Llanrwst. The main trail descends to Maenan Abbey Hotel then continues for 2 miles near the attractive river Conwy, before following minor roads back up the eastern side of the valley and continuing into Llanrwst, for a final short riverside section to the ancient bridge of Pont Fawr.

From Llanrwst the trail follows a scenic undulating route across attractive part wooded upland pasture offering good mountain views. It then visits the craggy top of Mynydd Garthmyn, another stunning viewpoint, before descending into the valley and crossing a suspension bridge over the Afon Conwy into Betws-y-Coed on probably the quietest approach to this visitor hot spot.

After leaving Betws-y-Coed by the Waterloo Bridge the trail climbs through areas of woodland on the eastern side of the valley, before offering a choice of interesting routes. One features the old upland droving village of Capel Garmon and an impressive Neolithic burial chamber, the other a delightful ancient track across attractive upland country adjoining the dominant crag of Dinas Mawr. Both routes then combine to descend in stages to Pont Rhydlanfair, an ancient stone bridge over the Afon Conwy. The trail now follows a scenic country road and a few available paths across enclosed upland pasture, part of the large former Penrhyn estate now owned by the National Trust. After enjoying extensive mountain views the trail descends to rejoin the Afon Conwy at Ysbyty Ifan, which takes its name from a hospice established here in the 12thC for travellers in need.

From Ysbyty Ifan the trail offers two routes to Penmachno. One takes the longer and more challenging approach following the river along the more rugged upper Conwy valley, past waterfalls, to its source at Llyn Conwy, owned by the National Trust. After passing round either side of this remote lake the trail descends to a minor upland road which it follows down a dramatic side valley before continuing along the lush Machno valley to Penmachno. This route is only suitable for experienced and well equipped hillwalkers who enjoy such a wild upland landscape, as part of it crosses demanding and largely pathless tussocky and heather Open Access land, rough underfoot. The easier and more direct alternative is to follow a delightful old drovers' route between the two ancient communities on scenic upland roads and a track, offering panoramic views, especially on the descent to Penmachno.

The next section follows the Afon Machno along the tributary valley, past an ancient packhorse bridge, waterfalls and where it joins the Afon Conwy by Conwy Falls. There is then a choice of routes to Betws-y-Coed. One heads west along the wooded Lledr valley, then climbs through woodland to Llyn Elsi, an attractive popular upland lake in Gwydwr Forest Park before descending to Betws-y-Coed. The other lower alternative visits the famous Fairy Glen, a deep narrow wooded Conwy river gorge, then follows a scenic road through woodland.

After a delightful section of riverside walking the trail leaves Betws-y-Coed and follows waymarked forest trails up through Gwydyr Forest Park to Llyn Parc, a large attractive lake hidden amongst the trees. From here there is a choice of interesting routes to Trefriw. One takes a longer, meandering undulating approach through Gwydyr Forest Park to its northern edge where it meets the foothills of the Carneddau, before following the wooded edge of Cwm Crafnant down to Trefriw. It features several scenic upland lakes – including popular Llyn Geirionydd and Llyn Crafnant – one of Snowdonia's hidden gems. The alternative easier and more direct route continues through the edge of Gwydyr Forest Park down to the valley, where it joins the Afon Conwy to reach Llanrwst. Later it continues beside the Afon Conwy then follows the Afon Crafnant to Trefriw.

After visiting woodland above Trefriw the trail follows a scenic upland road offering good views, then descends a path to cross the Afon Ddu. There is then a choice of routes down to Dolgarrog through the mature woodland of Coed Dolgarrog National Nature Reserve. One route first climbs to join a hillside pipeline offering extensive views, then descends the steep wooded hillside directly to Dolgarrog. The alternative makes an earlier descent then extends alongside the Afon Ddu to the Afon Conwy, before returning through woodland to Dolgarrog.

After a short informative trail commemorating the worst dam disaster in Wales the route continues up the valley to Llanbedr-y-cennin, then on to the hamlet of Pontwgan. From here there is a choice of interesting routes to Parc Mawr, attractive woodland owned by the Woodland Trust. One takes a long meandering approach featuring a 13thC church on the site of the Roman fort of Canovium, an historic crossing point of the Afon Conwy, then attractive undulating countryside. The alternative route takes a shorter more direct approach via Rowen, one of the prettiest villages in the Conwy Valley.

From Parc Mawr there is a choice of routes to Conwy. One follows an ancient highway up through attractive woodland then open hillside to remote St Celynin's church, one of the oldest in Snowdonia. It continues across open upland country near the foothills of North Snowdonia, enjoying extensive views. After reaching the historic Sychnant Pass it climbs onto Conwy Mountain, with its Iron Age hillfort, and makes a spectacular descent down its ridge towards Conwy. The alternative lower route passes through the edge of Parc Mawr, then heads more directly to Conwy via the village of Henryd, Conwy Touring Park and farmland offering great views of the river Conwy to reach a prominent close viewpoint of Conwy castle at the finish.

The final section, a circular walk, is full of interest and contrasts with other parts of the trail. After passing through the medieval town it heads along the estuary, visits Conwy Marina then continues past dunes to Conwy Bay. It then returns via the golf course and attractive woodland for an exhilarating walk along the medieval town walls to finish at Conwy quayside.

LLANDUDNO TO GLAN CONWY

12½ miles

1 Llandudno to Deganwy

7 miles

The first section of the Conwy Valley Way is a spectacular start to this long distance walk, offering close views of Great Orme's stunning limestone cliffs and birdlife and later breathtaking coastal and mountain views. From the North Shore the trail heads towards the pier to join Marine Drive, which it follows around this dramatic limestone headland up to Pen-y-Gogarth (Great Orme's Head), with its former lighthouse and roadside cafe. It then makes a long steady descent – offering the first view of the mouth of the Conwy estuary – to West Shore, then continues along its promenade to join a shoreline recreational route, known as the Conwy Estuary Trail, to Deganwy.

Llandudno, known as the 'Queen of Welsh resorts', lies on a peninsula between the impressive carboniferous limestone headlands of the Great and Little Orme. The name 'Orme' is said to derive from a Viking name for 'sea monster' – an apt description when viewed from sea! Llandudno (meaning 'enclosure' of Tudno) was named after Tudno, a 6thC Christian who built the first church in the area. This elegant town, largely built between 1849 and 1912 was purposely designed as a seaside resort, under the guidance of the wealthy Mostyn family. The town was laid out in a grid pattern that curved to reflect the sweep of the bay, with wide streets and attractive buildings. The arrival of the branch railway in 1858 ensured its development into the premier visitor destination it remains today. The Great Orme, which is now managed as a Country Park and Nature Reserve, is a SSSI, a Special Area of Conservation, and has Heritage Coast status. Its famous feral Kashmir goats, said to originate from a pair sent with others from India as a present for Queen Victoria, have been roaming wild here since the 1890s. Running around its cliffs, home to a variety of sea birds, is Marine Drive, a spectacular Victorian toll road, and rising to its summit (679 feet/207 metres) is Britain's only cable-hauled road tramway – both engineering marvels. There are many sites of historical and archaeological interest, including extensive Bronze Age copper mines.

1 The trail starts from the Cenotaph on North Shore promenade. *The wide promenade, built on a natural shingle bank, and the elegant hotels adjoining it were designed to create a classical frontage to the new resort.* After admiring the sweeping view towards the Little Orme, walk along the promenade towards the Great Orme, then follow the pier walkway behind the Grand Hotel (1901). *The current pier was built in 1876/7 to*

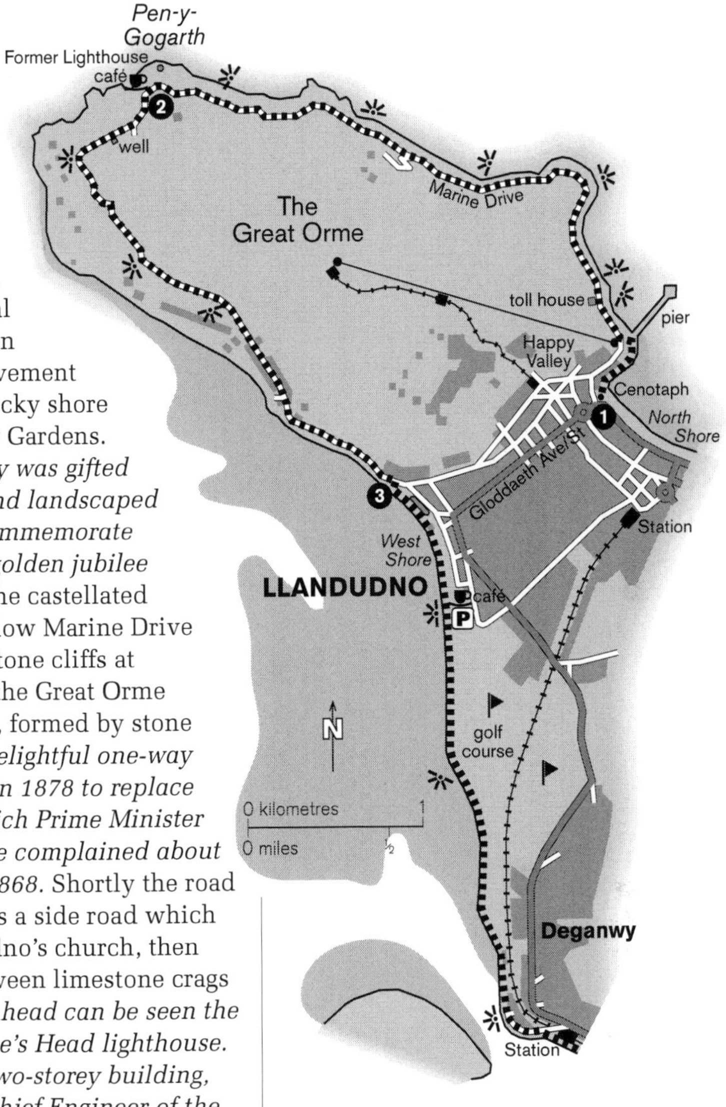

replace an earlier one destroyed in 1859 by a storm. It was later extended to the promenade, making it the longest in Wales at 2,295 feet. Turn through its original gated entrance then walk along the pavement overlooking the rocky shore past Happy Valley Gardens. *This former quarry was gifted by Lord Mostyn and landscaped into gardens to commemorate Queen Victoria's golden jubilee in 1887.* Go past the castellated toll house and follow Marine Drive beneath the limestone cliffs at the eastern tip of the Great Orme containing arches, formed by stone extraction. *This delightful one-way toll road opened in 1878 to replace an 1858 path, which Prime Minister William Gladstone complained about during a visit in 1868.* Shortly the road heads west, passes a side road which leads up to St Tudno's church, then rises steadily between limestone crags and steep cliffs. *Ahead can be seen the former Great Orme's Head lighthouse. This castellated two-storey building, designed by the Chief Engineer of the Mersey Docks and Harbour Board and set high on the steep cliffs, served as a lighthouse from 1862 until 1985, after which it became a unique bed and breakfast establishment. It is said to be haunted by the ghost of Austin, a former lighthouse keeper, who drowned trying to save a mariner.*

2 Eventually you reach the Rest and Be Thankful café, which may tempt you to stop. Continue along the road, shortly passing Ffynnon Gaseg (Mare's Well) – *which once serviced the passing horse-drawn carriages which originally took visitors along this scenic toll road.*

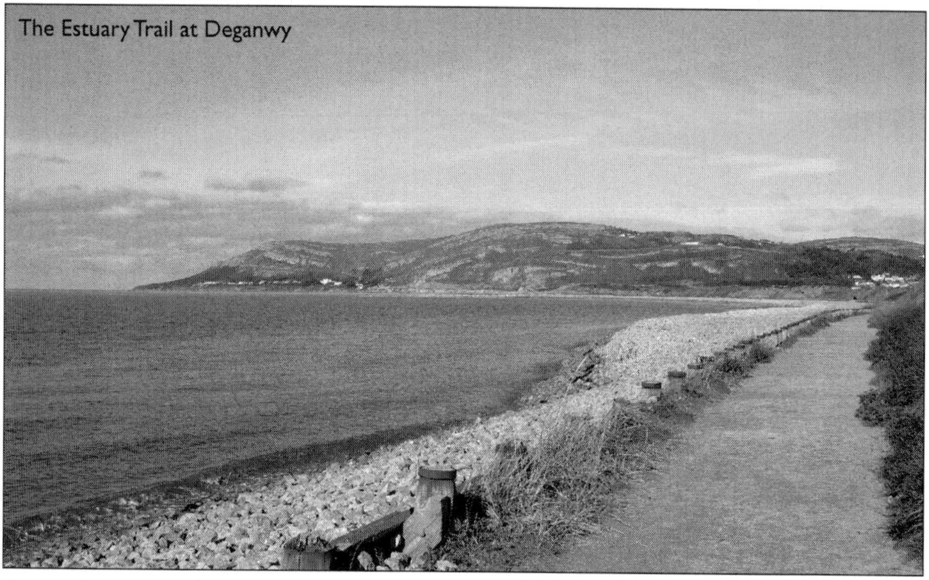

Soon afterwards the road bends south-east and begins a long steady descent beneath the limestone cliffs – *offering extensive new views across Conwy Bay to Anglesey and to the mouth of the Conwy estuary, with the distant Carneddau mountains beyond. Folklore has it that the sea hides the legendary lands of Helig which disappeared under the waters in the 6thC. On a shelf beneath Marine Drive is an area known as the Gunsite, where the Royal Artillery ran Officer Cadet courses in gunnery, wireless and searchlight skills from 1941. At its peak this peaceful green coastal site housed 745 people of various ranks and ran up to 14 courses. Little now remains of this once important and bustling wartime facility.* Eventually you pass another castellated toll house.

3 Shortly go along the promenade at West Shore. *It is hard to believe that this was once an industrial area for sorting ore from the Great Orme copper mine. The ore was washed in a pool here in the mid-19thC, which was later developed into the model boating pool.* Go past the White Rabbit Statue – *erected in 1933 to promote the town's association with Alice Liddell, the inspiration for Lewis Carrol's Alice in Wonderland, who reputedly spent several summers nearby with her family from 1861* – and the model boating pool. Continue along the promenade – *with the two small peaks ahead marking the site of Deganwy Castle* – to a car park, with a café nearby. Now follow the wide shoreline Conwy Estuary Trail beneath dunes and a golf course – *enjoying fine views to Conwy mountain, along the coast to Penmaenmawr, and across to Anglesey.* Eventually you join a shoreline road in Deganwy at the narrowest part of the mouth of the Conwy estuary.

2 Deganwy to Glan Conwy

5½ miles

The trail now passes Deganwy Quay Marina and continues along the edge of the estuary, with a good view across to Conwy and its castle, to Conwy Nature Reserve. Here it incorporates a delightful but optional nearly two mile walk exploring the RSPB wetland reserve, with its Visitor Centre, shop and café, plus viewing screens and hides providing opportunities for watching birds on its two main lagoons. Created out of mud extracted during the building of the road tunnel under the Conwy estuary, the reserve now provides an important habitat for a variety of birds and other wildlife. There is a small entrance charge for non RSPB members, but well worth it. Afterwards the trail passes through nearby Llandudno Junction, then follows a designated walkway under the A55 and continues past a good viewpoint into Llansantffraidd Glan Conwy as its full name is known.

The twin hills above Deganwy, known as Vardre, which have probably been occupied since Roman times, have witnessed centuries of settlement and warfare. During the 6th and 9thC, a castle for Maelgwyn Gwynedd, occupied this site. In 1078, a new Norman castle was built here by Robert of Rhuddlan. During the 13thC Deganwy was a focus of the campaigns by the English Kings to exert control over Wales. In 1215, the castle was rebuilt by Llywelyn ap Iorwerth after successfully regaining land lost to King John, and after some years of peace, it withstood a siege by Henry III in 1245, but by 1257 was in English control. Walls and towers were constructed, encompassing both hills, but the castle was retaken and destroyed by Llywelyn ap Gruffyd (the Last) in 1263. When English control over Wales was finally established in 1284, Edward I decided to build a new castle across the river at Conwy.

For centuries, until Telford's suspension bridge was opened in 1826, a ferry operated across the tidal river from here. A new river taxi service to Conwy began here in 2010. The arrival of the branch railway in the 1850s led to the development of Deganwy into a small fashionable resort, and later a commercial dock for the exporting of slate brought by rail from the quarries at Blaenau Ffestiniog. During the 20thC the dock fell into decline and dereliction. Recent years have seen the former slate wharfs being developed into the prestigious Deganwy Quay complex, with its marina, housing and hotel, which opened in 2006.

1 At the railway crossing go past the rear of toilets and continue with the estuary trail – *with a good view across to Conwy Marina.* After passing Deganwy Quay the trail continues above the edge of the estuary – *enjoying good views to Conwy and its impressive castle.* Eventually you reach a monument to commemorate the opening of the Conwy tunnel by the Queen in 1991. Just beyond at an information board the walkway splits. (The right-hand one passes through gardens, then crosses the bridge over the river to enter Conwy – an

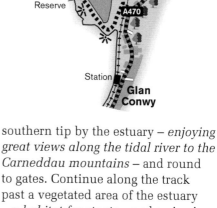

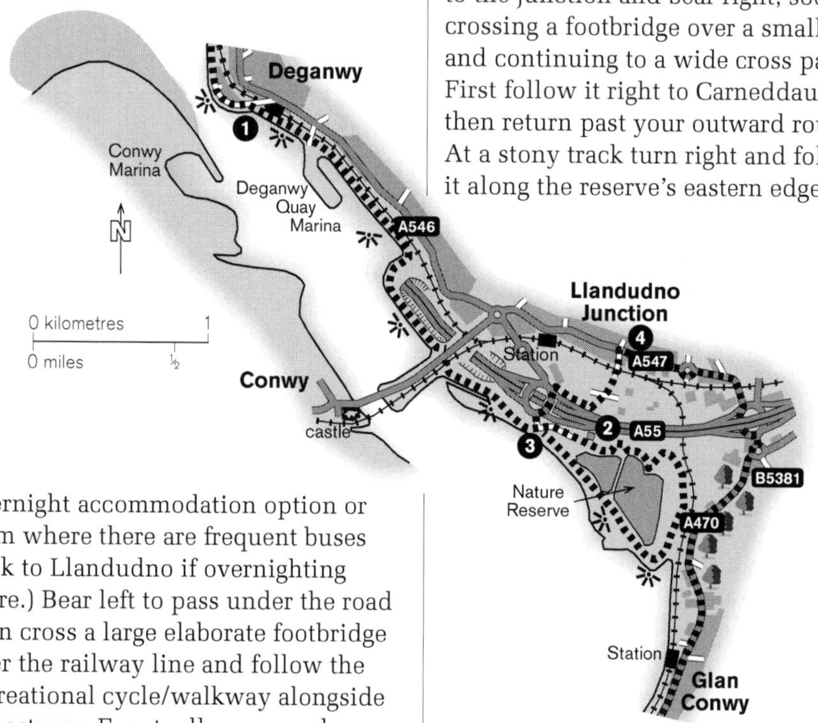

overnight accommodation option or from where there are frequent buses back to Llandudno if overnighting there.) Bear left to pass under the road then cross a large elaborate footbridge over the railway line and follow the recreational cycle/walkway alongside the estuary. Eventually you reach the bend of an access road which leads to the nearby RSPB Conwy Nature Reserve. Follow the road to the Visitor Centre. (If not wishing to include the walk around the Nature Reserve simply resume instructions in paragraph 3.)

2 From a door at the far end of the Visitor Centre follow a stony path to a nearby cafe and toilets. Just beyond the path splits. Keep ahead and follow the boardwalked path through bulrushes, past a path on the right, soon bending left to a path junction. Turn right. At another junction turn right signposted to the hides. At the next junction take the right fork to Tal-y-fan hide. Return to the junction and bear right, soon crossing a footbridge over a small pond and continuing to a wide cross path. First follow it right to Carneddau hide then return past your outward route. At a stony track turn right and follow it along the reserve's eastern edge to its southern tip by the estuary – *enjoying great views along the tidal river to the Carneddau mountains* – and round to gates. Continue along the track past a vegetated area of the estuary – *a habitat for stoats* – and a viewing screen then nearby Benarth hide, to eventually reach the reserve's access road.

3 Go up the access road to the large roundabout. Turn right along the pavement, cross the slip road then follow the pavement across the bridge over the A55. Cross the next slip road and go down a stepped railed path. Continue along the wide hard surfaced enclosed path parallel with the nearby slip road. At its end turn left along a

stony path to a road at the industrial estate. Go up the path opposite to a kissing gate onto a rough access lane by houses. Continue ahead to cross a bridge over the railway line and follow the road past houses to the main road in Llandudno Junction.

4 Follow the road right through Llandudno Junction, later bending right over the railway line. As you approach the large roundabout beneath the A55 follow the walkway/cycleway round to cross the slip road, then under the A55 road bridge. After crossing the next slip road follow the walkway/cycleway left round to a small roundabout by a Shell garage. Continue along the pavement beside the A470. Later divert into a lay-by with seats to enjoy a great view overlooking the RSPB Nature Reserve, to Conwy Castle, and along the river estuary with its backcloth of mountains. Continue into the dormer village of Llansantffraidd Glan Conwy passing Snowdonia Nurseries and the Business Park to reach the entrance to the railway halt on the Conwy Valley line.

GLAN CONWY TO LLANRWST

14½ or 13 miles

3 Glan Conwy to Graig

4½ miles

The trail now begins its passage along the eastern side of the Conwy Valley. After leaving Glan Conwy it crosses peaceful countryside on quiet roads and field paths, featuring good views across the river and an ancient burial chamber. It then follows quiet minor roads offering extensive views on an undulating meandering route through attractive countryside to a side valley, only ¼ mile from Bodnant Gardens, one of Britain's most beautiful gardens managed by the National Trust, which you may wish to visit before continuing to the nearby hamlet of Graig.

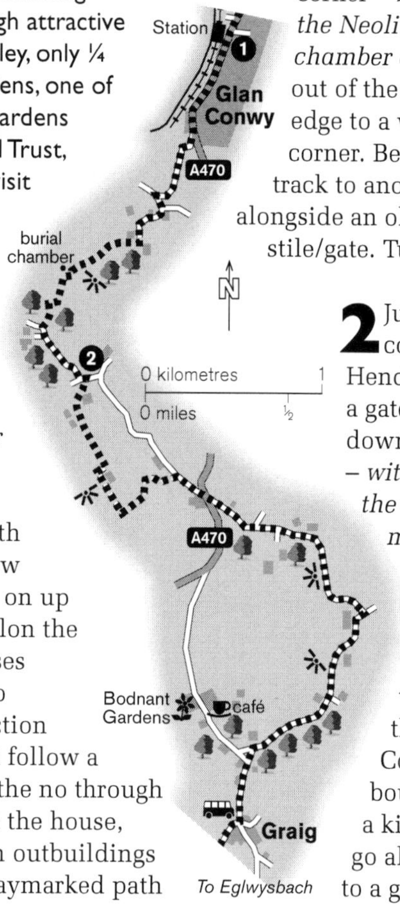

1 Go past The Estuary pub and continue along the A470 (Llanrwst road) – *soon passing another good viewpoint across the estuary.* At the end of houses go down Garth Road. Follow the narrow road over a stream and on up past houses. After Awelon the road climbs again, passes further houses and a no through road. At a junction by Garth turn right and follow a signposted path down the no through road. At its end go past the house, then turn right between outbuildings and follow a narrow waymarked path along the bottom edge of a small wood. When it splits keep with the higher path alongside the fence through the edge of the wood to a kissing gate in the wood corner. Continue ahead across the mid-slopes of the large field – *enjoying good views of the river and Tal-y-fan ahead* – to a kissing gate into a small area of woodland. Follow the waymarked path down to the fence corner – *beyond which stands the Neolithic portal burial chamber of Allor Moloch* – then out of the trees and along a field edge to a waymarked gate in the corner. Bear right along a green track to another gate, then turn left alongside an old boundary down to a stile/gate. Turn left up the road.

2 Just past the stone columned entrance to Hendre Waelod go through a gate up on the right. Go down the access track – *with a good view across the river to the Carneddau mountains* – then when it bends down towards a house keep ahead along grass to a kissing gate. Follow the path to a stile, then to another ahead. Continue beside the boundary to go through a kissing gate in it, then go along the top field edge to a gate in the corner. Now

View across the RSPB Reserve to Conwy Castle

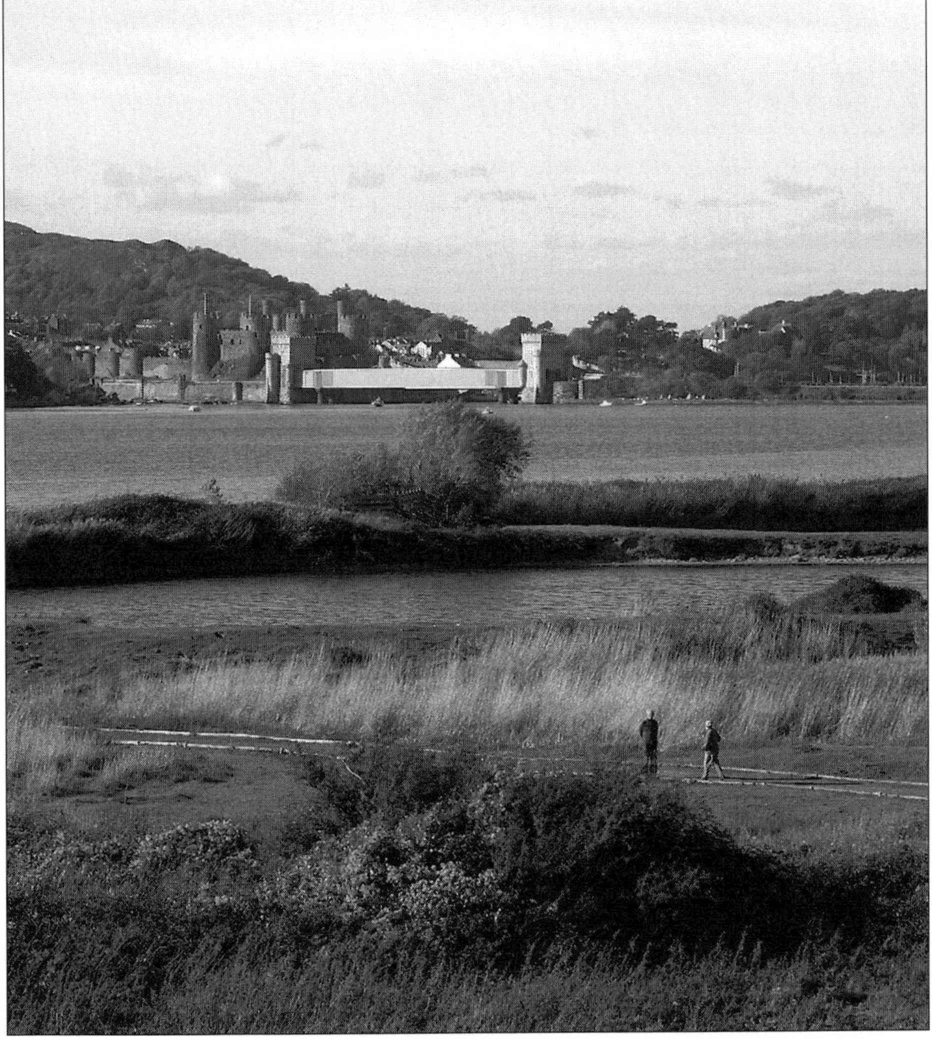

follow a stony access track down and past Aberconwy Barn and Tyn-y-Coed – *with a good view ahead of the bend of the river.* Follow the access track up to a road, then follow it right to the A470. Go down Ffordd Prenol opposite, soon rising and passing Ffordd Meusydd. The road rises steadily, later levelling out and offering extensive views. At the junction turn right (signposted to Eglwysbach) past a farm, after which the road makes a long steady descent. After levelling out it splits. (For Bodnant Gardens take the right fork.) Take the left fork, then at the junction turn left into the small hamlet of Graig.

4 Graig to Maenan

5 miles

This section offers great variety and good views along the Conwy Valley. The route follows minor country roads across part wooded upland pasture, past a remote lake, reaching a height of 590 feet/180 metres. It then follows woodland paths to the dramatic viewpoint of Cadair Ifan Goch crag, owned by the National Trust, before descending to the small rural community of Maenan.

1 At the crossroads turn right past the bus shelter and go along Fford Ty Gwyn. Follow it down past cottages into the valley to cross over the river. Continue up the road past a no through road and a farm on the left, then a road on the right. The road now climbs steadily before levelling out at a good viewpoint looking across the bend of the river. Turn left up Ffordd Llyn Syberi. The road climbs steadily – *later with good views north along the river to Deganwy and the Ormes, then across to the Carneddau mountains.* After passing Ty Newydd the road levels out and continues along the part wooded upland farmland grazed by sheep, passing Meddiant Uchaf. Shortly the road descends then passes alongside the attractive lake of Llyn Syberi. Continue along the road past Caedoeg, Hafodty, and another small lake amongst trees, then beneath Pen-Or – *enjoying good views down to the Afon Conwy and across to Dolgarrog with the Carneddau mountains beyond.* The road then descends and continues to a junction. Go down the road ahead, then turn left along a side road to Plas Iwrwg. Go through a small wooden gate by double gates just beyond the garage. Cross the stony parking area towards the gable end of the house, then descend steps to another small gate. Go along the left-hand field edge beside the tree boundary, through a gap in the corner. Mid-way across the next field angle

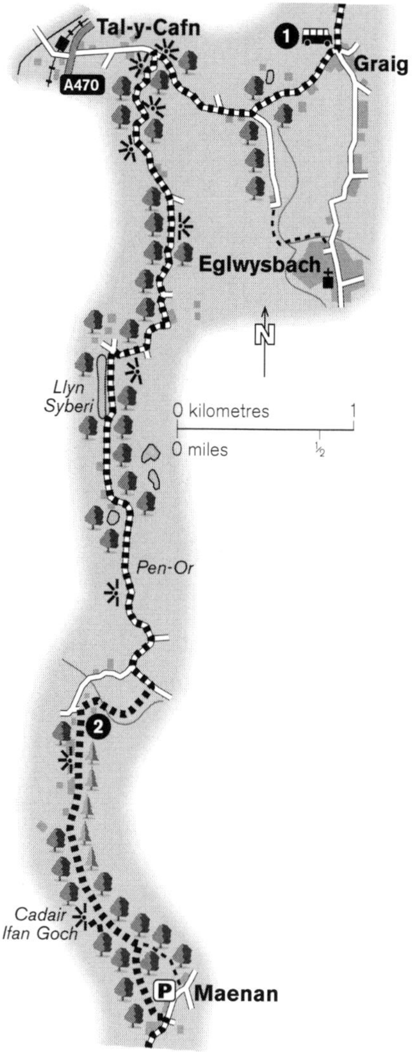

View from Cadair Ifan Goch

right to walk along the bottom field edge above the stream to go through a kissing gate on the left about 10 yards below a dam. Bear right above the stream to a kissing gate/gate. Go past a barn and a derelict cottage to a gate. Follow the hedge-lined green track to another gate.

2 Turn left up an access track passing behind a cottage, and soon two further cottages – *with a good view over the Conwy valley.* Continue along the track's left fork (Llidiart y Coed) rising steadily beneath the wooded slope. Just before the garage continue on the wide path along the edge of the wood, soon narrowing and continuing above a boundary. After a kissing gate follow the path ahead through woodland, soon rising steadily then descending to a path junction at a National Trust board. Here turn sharp right to follow the path through the trees and up onto the narrow crag of Cadair Ifan Goch – *offering a superb view along the Conwy valley. According to local legend Cadair Ifan Goch (Red Ifan's seat) used to sit here to cool his feet in the Conwy river. Another legend says he stood astride the river, one foot here and one on Pen-y-Gaer opposite bending to wash his face in the river below.* Retrace your steps then continue with the main path to where it splits. (If you intend following the higher road route to Llanrwst take the left fork down through the wood to a small car park at a road junction and nearby primary school at Maenan. Go along the road ahead.) Take the right fork down through the wood to join an access track to reach the nearby road by Capel Soar.

5 Maenan to Llanrwst

5 or 3½ miles

The trail now descends to Maenan Abbey (where refreshments are available) and continues along a 2 mile section of embanked path near the attractive river Conwy. Afterwards the route follows minor roads back up the eastern side of the valley and on into Llanrwst for a final short riverside section to the ancient bridge of Pont Fawr. If time is pressing or you wish to maintain height, an alternative route is to simply follow minor roads south from Maenan as shown to join the main route at point 2.

1 Turn right and follow the narrow road down the wooded hillside to a junction above a narrow wooded valley. Follow the road right down beside the valley and its cascading river to the A470 by Maenan Abbey Hotel. *It takes its name from the Cistercian Abbey that once occupied the site. In 1283 Edward I required an existing monastery to move from the site that had been chosen for his planned castle and walled town at Conwy, and he subsequently financed the building of a new Abbey here at Maenan. The Abbey became a powerful body until its dissolution by Henry VIII in 1537. The Wynn family built a house on the site in 1599 which in the 1850s was replaced by the current building, now a hotel.* Cross the road and follow the signposted path through the entrance opposite (Coach House etc.) After passing the interesting houses continue to a gate, then cross a footbridge over the river to a nearby kissing gate. Go along the embanked riverside path, cross the railway line (heed the warning signs) and continue to where the river joins the Afon Conwy. The embanked path, part of a flood protection scheme, now more or less follows the course of the river close to the western wooded side of the valley. Later, after a view across to Trefriw, it bends east away from the river, briefly rejoining it. Cross the railway and with care the A470 beyond. Follow the signposted

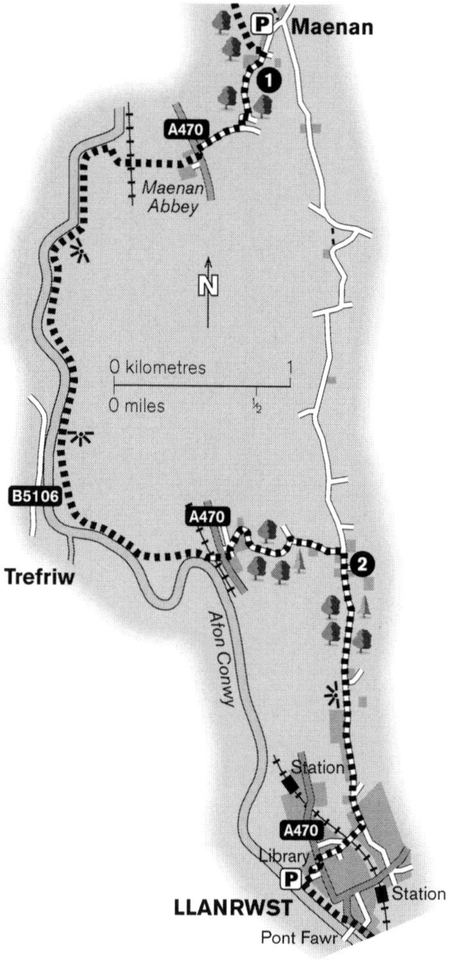

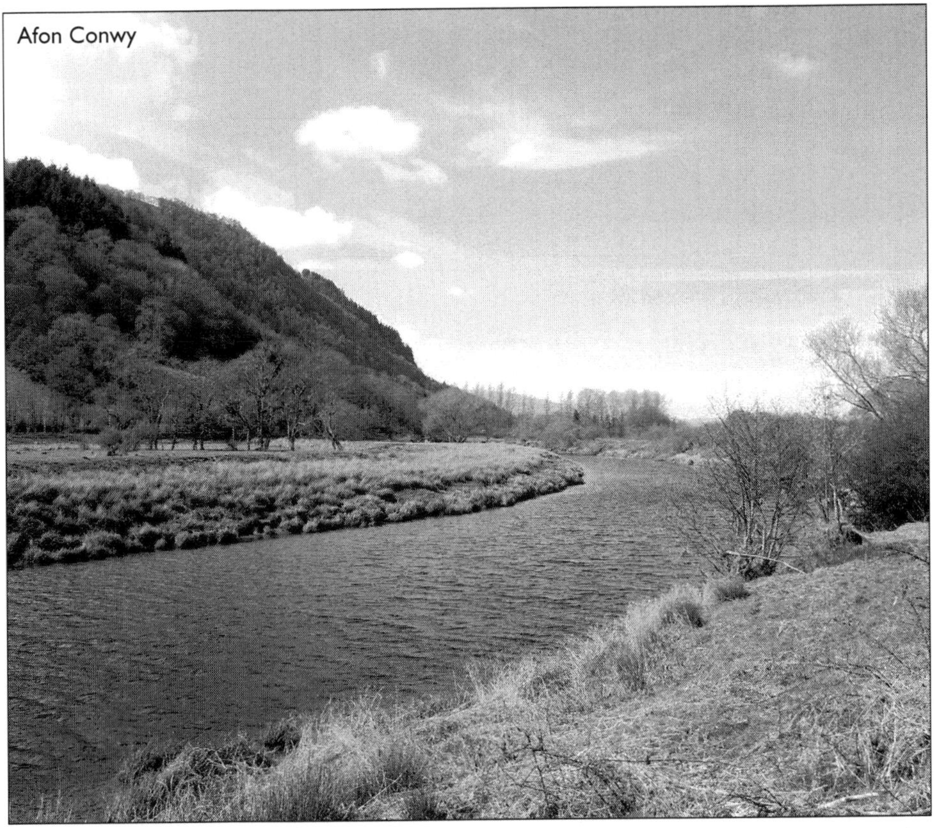

gated footpath to the former main road nearby. Turn left past cottages and at the crossroads turn right up the side road (Llandoged) past more cottages, then a small caravan site to eventually reach a T-junction. Turn right.

2 Go along the road, passing a side road, after which the road descends past exposed limestone crags in woodland. Continue along the road through the outskirts of Llanrwst, then turn right along Ffordd Pari past the cattle market, over a the railway and past a chapel. At the T-junction turn left then cross the road into Plas yn dre. Follow the road past the library and through the car park to descend steps onto the riverbank. Now follow the riverside path to join the road near Pont Fawr. *This elegant narrow three arch stone bridge was designed by the famous architect Inigo Jones and built in 1636, at an expense of £1,000, shared jointly by Caernarfon and Denbigh counties. It replaced an existing ford and was the first bridge across the river. Built for horses and carts it has survived battles, modern traffic and regular floods. On the other side stands Ty Hwnt i'r Bont, a 15thC cottage, which became a 16thC courthouse and is now a tea room owned by the National Trust.*

LLANRWST TO BETWS-Y-COED

9 miles

This next section follows a scenic undulating route featuring a classic crag viewpoint. Despite being only 9 miles it takes longer than you think (6-7 hours) and will be sufficient for most people, allowing time to explore Betws-y-Coed. However, before descending to Betws-y-Coed it is possible to extend into the early part of the next section, then descend off the trail to the Conwy Falls café, where you can catch the no. 64 bus to Betws-y-Coed, making 10¼ miles in total, then returning by bus the next day.

Llanrwst, standing at an important crossing of the Afon Conwy, is first mentioned as the site of a bloody Welsh battle in 954 AD. This ancient market town, which takes its name from the 6thC St Grwst, is known for the making of harps and clocks, and in the 19thC, the spinning of woollen yarn and the knitting of stockings. For a time Llanrwst was one of the largest towns in Wales and had a small harbour on its northern side. It still serves as the market town for the Conwy Valley. Its attractions include Almshouses (1610), now a local museum, the parish church of St Grwst (1470), and in its grounds the 17thC Gwydir Chapel. This mausoleum, built for the Wynn family from nearby Gwydir Castle, contains part of the stone sarcophagus which once contained the body of the Welsh Prince Llywelyn the Great. Interestingly Llanrwst has two railway stations. Llanrwst North was originally known as Llanrwst and Trefriw station when the railway arrived in 1863, as it was also meant to cater for visitors to the spa village of Trefriw on the western side of the valley.

6 Llanrwst to Coed Newydd

4½ miles

The trail leaves Llanrwst and passes through Coed Garth then follows an undulating route across attractive part wooded upland pasture, with good mountain views, to reach Coed Newydd.

1 From Pont Fawr go along the pavement above the river, then continue along the pavement opposite. After crossing the railway line, continue past the graveyard, then turn left along a side road past the B5427 (Nebo Road). Just beyond a bus stop take a signposted path along a narrow access lane on the right between houses. Pass between the rear of houses and garages, then follow a green track past gardens to a stile. Go along the field edge to a stile onto an access lane. Go along the fenced path opposite to a stile, then continue along edge of two fields by a stream past the nearby school to a small metal gate into Coed y Garth. Cross the footbridge over the stream and follow a path angling left up through trees. When it levels out bear left to follow a track up through mixed woodland, shortly

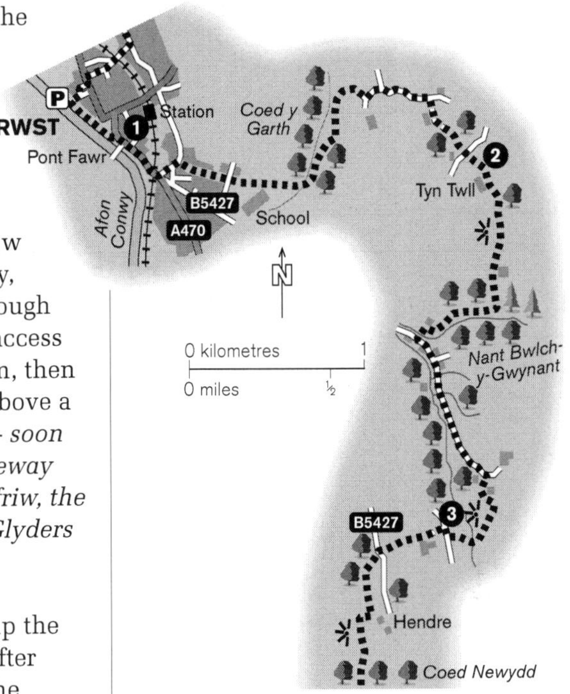

bending right to join a track at the wood corner. Turn left along the hedge-lined track to a gate. Just beyond, where you are joined by another track, bear right. At an access road turn left. At the junction turn right up the narrow road past a small wooded valley, then take a signposted path through a gate on the right. Follow the access track to Garth-yr-Hwylbren farm, then bear left to a kissing gate/gate above a stream. Continue up the track – *soon with a good view through a gateway across the Conwy Valley to Trefriw, the Carneddau range, Tryfan, the Glyders and Moel Siabod* – to a road.

2 Follow a signposted path up the access track to Tyn Twll. After passing the farm continue up the track – *enjoying extensive views.* Go past farm buildings and through a waymarked gate ahead. Go down the path and on to a gate, then follow the green track down the wood, soon bending right and continuing down through the trees above Nant Bwlch-y-gwynt to a gate. Continue down the track, pass between farm buildings, then cross a footbridge over the river just before the house. Go across the field to a kissing gate onto an access drive and the adjoining minor road. Turn left along the road past houses and a side road, then follow the no through road up the delightful wooded valley. The road rises steadily past Ty Newydd, then above an old cottage. Take a signposted path along the access track to Ty Mawr, then go through a waymarked gate at the far end of its outbuilding. Go along an old hedged/tree-lined green track, soon bending left. It continues between walls, then descends to a gate by a wood corner. Follow the track down beside the wood to another gate, then cross a footbridge over the river. Follow the track up to a road.

3 Turn right then left on a signposted path along Fedw's access track. Go past a bungalow then a house and through a gate ahead between outbuildings. Go past the large barn, then bear right, through a gate and on to go through another gate ahead. Turn left and head down the large field – *enjoying extensive views along the valley to Llanrwst* – soon descending alongside a small wooded

valley to an old iron ladder-stile onto the road. Turn right, and do a sharp U-turn left along an access track to ornate entrance gates, then take a waymarked path over an old iron ladder-stile on the right. Follow the wide path down through the wood, soon levelling out – *offering a good view along the valley to Betws-y-Coed* – then joining a track. Go through a kissing gate by a gate just before Hendre House, then follow the waymarked path down beside the fence and up to a gate. Turn right and follow an old green track across the hillside to cross a stream and ladder-stile into Coed Newydd.

7 Coed Newydd to Betws-y-Coed railway station

4½ miles

The trail descends through the attractive woodland of Coed Newydd, then later rises through the mixed woodland of Coed Hafod before continuing across enclosed upland pasture to a minor road. Here it makes a rewarding diversion to a renowned viewpoint on Mynydd Garthmyn overlooking Betws-y-Coed, then up to its rocky summit (823 feet/251 metres) for superb all-round views. Afterwards the trail descends to the A470, then continues to a suspension bridge over the Afon Conwy to suddenly emerge in Betws-y-Coed, with the railway station nearby.

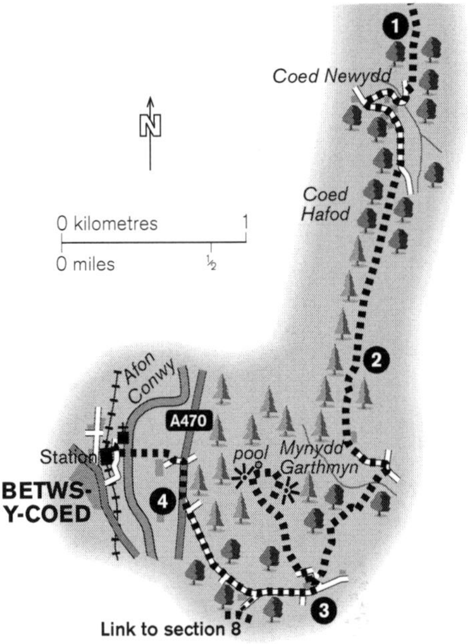

1 Take the path angling right through the wood down to a stile above Oaklands and on to join its driveway. Follow it over the river and along the edge of the wood to a road. Turn left up the road past cottages, then on a bend take a signposted path over a ladder-stile above a gate. Go up the field on a faint green track to a ladder-stile/gate in a wall into Coed Hafod. At a path junction just beyond follow the waymarked path leading left. It rises through the wood near a wall to a kissing gate at the wall/fence corner. The path continues up through the wood beside a fence, then up the wood edge to a ladder-stile. Go up a green track alongside the wood, passing through a gate.

2 Shortly go through a gate on the right. Just beyond turn left and follow a wide path through the conifers to a stile. Angle slightly right down the field – *ahead lies the rocky top of Mynydd Garthmyn* – to a post, then turn left down a path through gorse to a gate by a wall corner. Go past farm buildings and the house, then follow its access track to a road. Here go through a kissing gate on the right and down the edge of the field to cross a ladder-stile and stream. Follow the path through the wood to cross a ladder-stile. Turn left and follow the field edge round to cross a ladder-stile by a gate. Follow the fence on your left to another ladder-stile then go along a farm track beyond. Shortly cross an access lane by a garage to reach a kissing gate by a cottage and a road.

3 At the kissing gate turn right, go up steps and past Garmonfa, then turn left along the access track to a ladder-stile at the entrance to Pen-y-

Suspension bridge, Betws-y-Coed

Foel. Briefly follow its access track, then take a waymarked path on the right. It passes through an area of birch, rowan, bracken, heather and gorse to a stile – *offering good views of Moel Siabod, the Glyders, Tryfan and the Carneddau Mountains.* A few yards beyond angle left to follow a wide path up the slope, then after 15 yards take a narrow path angling left and continuing north to the left of a small rocky ridge to reach a small pool. Go up onto the nearby crag to a superb viewpoint – *north along the valley and down to Betws-y-Coed.* Afterwards go past the southern end of the pool, up the slope ahead, then up a path angling left. When the path levels out – *with a view of wind turbines ahead* – work your way up to a visible waymark post onto the impressive rocky summit of Mynydd Garthmyn, aptly named Picnic Point, for superb all-round views. Descend south-west, passing a group of trees to your right, to join your outward route. Return to the kissing gate at point **3**. Turn right down the road – *soon passing a signposted path on the left giving access to the next section of the trail if you wish to finish at Conwy Falls café* – after which the road continues down above a wooded valley to eventually reach the A470.

4 Cross the road with care and turn right along the roadside pathway, then turn left down the driveway to Muriau. Follow the waymarked path past the side of outbuildings to a small gate and on to cross a small elegant suspension bridge over the river Conwy into Betws-y-Coed. *It was built in 1930, after the destruction by floods of a bridge constructed by the Royal Engineers in WWI as a replacement for stepping stones just downstream.* At the road by the former parish church of St Michael's, dating from the 14thC, turn right then go through a staggered gate on the left and follow the pathway past the Buffet Coach café and nearby Conwy Valley railway shop and museum round to cross a footbridge over the railway line. Go along the platform to exit the station to reach the road beyond. *The extensive station buildings built in 1868 have been developed into shops and cafés.*

BETWS-Y-COED TO YSBYTY IFAN

7½ or 7 miles

8 Betws-y-Coed to Pont Rhydlanfair

4½ or 4 miles

After leaving Betws-y-Coed by the Waterloo Bridge the trail climbs through areas of woodland, before offering a choice of interesting routes to Penrhyddion Uchaf. Slightly longer **Route A** continues up to the upland old droving village of Capel Garmon (721 feet/220 metres), then visits an impressive Neolithic burial chamber before descending to a minor road. **Route B** features a delightful old track across attractive upland country adjoining the dominant crag of Dinas Mawr. Both routes combine to descend in stages by field paths and road to Pont Rhydlanfair, an ancient stone bridge over the Afon Conwy.

Betws-y-Coed, lying in a beautiful wooded valley near the confluence of the Llugwy and Conwy rivers, is the popular gateway into Snowdonia National Park. Romans once passed by on the Sarn Helen road which crosses the A5 near the inclined Miners bridge. Betws-y-Coed means 'Prayer house in the wood' and was founded around a church or a monastery in the 6thC. After Thomas Telford's Waterloo Bridge over the Conwy opened in 1815, the hitherto small community became an important staging post on the London to Holyhead Irish Mail coach road. During the 19thC its stunning scenery, including the famous Swallow Falls, attracted many eminent travellers,visitors and artists by road and later by railway. It further developed due to intensive lead-mining in Gwydyr Forest. In the mid 19thC a few people were engaged in the spinning of woollen yarn and the knitting of stockings. It remains North Wales's most popular inland resort and walking centre, attracting visitors throughout the year.

1 From the railway station follow the road left past a car park and toilets to the main road in Betws-y-Coed (A5). Cross to the other side and follow the road left through Betws-y-coed to Waterloo Bridge. *This attractively decorated cast-iron bridge includes an inscription celebrating the famous victory at Waterloo in 1815, the year it was built to carry the London-Holyhead road. Prior to this mail coaches had to pass this point and continue to Llanrwst to cross the river before returning south on the current B5106 to reach Betws-y-Coed.* Follow the pavement round alongside the A5, then take a signposted stepped path opposite past the end of Ty Gwyn – *a 16thC coaching inn.* The narrow walled path rises steadily through woodland, crosses a track, then

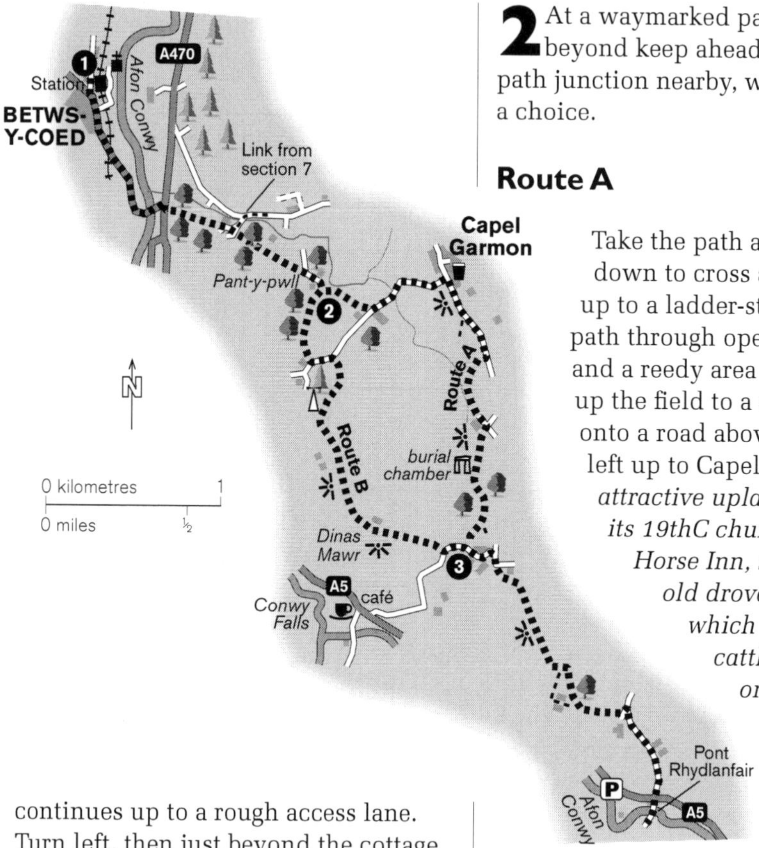

continues up to a rough access lane. Turn left, then just beyond the cottage turn right through a wall gap onto another track to cross a nearby ladder-stile. The path rises steadily through the wood to leave it by another ladder-stile, then goes up the field edge to a stile. Continue up the waymarked path, soon bending right up to a stone stile above a gate. Follow the waymarked path up reed/tree/bracken covered ground to a kissing gate. The path continues beside a wall then rises to join a driveway. Follow it down to Pant-y-pwll boarding kennels/cattery. Pass between buildings then bend right to an old iron gate at the end of an old building.

2 At a waymarked path junction beyond keep ahead to another path junction nearby, where you have a choice.

Route A

Take the path angling left down to cross a stream and on up to a ladder-stile. Follow the path through open woodland and a reedy area to a gate. Go up the field to a small iron gate onto a road above. Follow it left up to Capel Garmon. *This attractive upland village, with its 19thC church and White Horse Inn, stands on an old drovers' route along which sheep and cattle once passed on their way to market at Llanrwst or further afield in England.* Turn right along the road out of the village – *enjoying good views west to Moel Siabod, the Glyders and the Carneddau mountains.* After passing two access tracks the road begins to rise. Take a signposted Snowdonia National Park path through a kissing gate on the right. Follow the waymarked path alongside the boundary to a kissing gate and on to pass through Tyn-y-Coed farm. Go up its access lane. On the bend turn right down to a finger post and through a nearby small gate. Go along the field edge, and through a gate in the boundary. Angle left across the field to reach the burial chamber. Go through a nearby kissing gate, then about 30 yards beyond angle left up to a waymark post on the small rocky ridge. Continue up through trees and on to a finger post. Turn right down a green track to a gate. Continue down the track, then follow the signposted diverted path down the slope to a minor road. Turn left.

Route B

Keep ahead beneath a tree-encrusted crag and on near the wall. At a finger post bear left and follow the path through an area of gorse to a ladder-stile. Follow the enclosed path down, past a stile in the wood corner, to a stile ahead onto a road. Follow it left. Just before a gate across the road, turn right on a signposted path up a green track near the wall to a gate at the wood corner. Continue up the green track and on alongside the wood's perimeter wall, soon passing a radio transmitter mast near the wood corner. Continue for ¾ mile along the gated green track across scenic undulating rugged upland pasture – *enjoying extensive valley and mountain views* – past the nearby bracken covered rocky top of Dinas Mawr and on down to a minor road. Follow it left up to join Route A.

3 Follow the road up to pass between Penrhyddion Uchaf and Penrhyddion Canol. Continue up the road – *offering good mountain views and along Cwm Penmachno* – soon bending right. When it bends left towards cottages turn right across a parking area to a small wooden gate. Turn left, then right down past gorse. Go through a small metal gate on the left below an outbuilding then through the large gate ahead beneath the house. Go along the field edge, through a facing gate and across the next field to a gate ahead. Go across the next large field. Midway angle right to a kissing gate in the corner. Go across the large field – *enjoying a good view along Cwm Penmachno* – to a gate in the bottom right hand corner. Follow a track past the stone barn and through a facing gate ahead. (The Right of Way follows the track down to Carreg-coediog Farm, but the next section follows a waymarked permissive National Trust path which avoids going through it.) Just beyond angle left off the track past a waymark post at the fence corner. Go across open ground to pass between gorse, then follow cables to another waymark post at a fence ahead just to the right of a telegraph pole. From its nearby corner continue down beside the fence to a gate at the bottom by an outbuilding at Carreg-coediog. Turn left to cross a stream and stone stile, then follow the fence on your right up to a gate by an outbuilding of Bancog farm. Follow its access track down to the road. Turn right and follow the road down to the A5. Cross to the road opposite. (At a lay-by 100 yards right along the road is a tea bar.)

9 Pont Rhydlanfair to Ysbyty Ifan

3 miles

The trail now follows a scenic country road and a few available paths through part of the National Trust's Ysbyty Estate. Later, after enjoying extensive mountain views, it descends to Ysbyty Ifan standing on a network of ancient routes.

1 Cross the stylish 18thC single arched stone bridge over the river Conwy. Continue up the road past a side road and follow the road south east – *with good views across the valley.* Follow the road past a farm, the entrance to Bryn Glas, Fron Ddu and Pen-y-geulan. Go past a road on the right then on the next bend keep ahead down a rough track past a cottage and over the river. Cross a raised stile ahead, then go up a depression in the field to an old wall. Follow the old embanked boundary left up to a stile/gate. Go up the field to a gate in the corner onto a road. Turn left up the road past a side road. It rises steadily giving good views west.

2 Just before the road bends right at a great all-round viewpoint – *north west to Snowdon, Moel Siabod, the Glyders, Tryfan, and the Carneddau mountains , north east to Mynydd Hiraethog, and southwards to the long bare ridge leading to Carnedd y Filiast, and the Arenigs further west* – go through a gate set back on the right on a signposted path. Follow the old enclosed green track, which is later sunken and reedy, up to a gate. Continue along the embankment

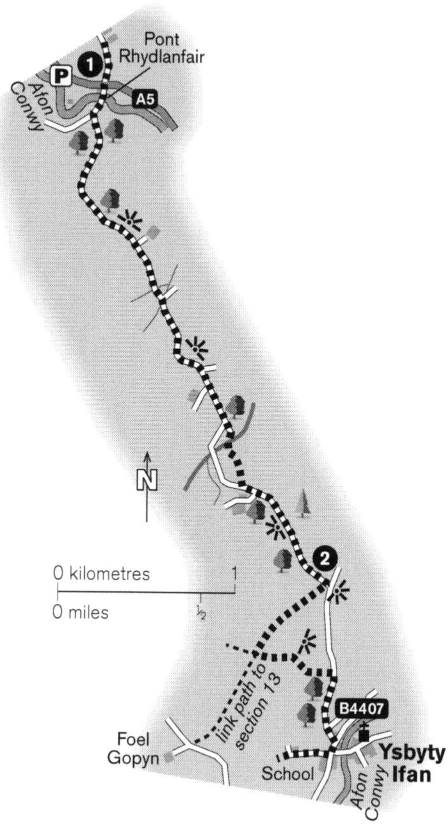

above the old reedy track to reach a waymark post just past a wall corner. (If time is pressing and Penmachno is your intended destination continue along the embanked path to a gate, then follow the old green track to an open gateway and on across rough upland pasture to the minor road near the entrance to Foel Gopyn, where you join the old drovers' route.) Here turn left across reedy ground to a kissing gate in the boundary corner. Descend the field edge to a stile, then the next field – *enjoying extensive views along the Conwy valley and south west to the Arenigs* – to a stile/gate. Descend the

next field edge to another stile/gate at a wood corner to rejoin the road below. Follow it down to Ysbyty Ifan, where you rejoin the Afon Conwy.

Ysbyty Ifan is an small attractive and historic Welsh speaking village set within land that formed part of the large Penrhyn estate, now owned by the National Trust. It lies at a crossing point of the Conwy river on a network of ancient routes to Anglesey, Bardsey, Mid-Wales, Chester and London, used by drovers, travellers and pilgrims. In this sheltered valley, known as Dogynwal, the Hospitaler Knights of St John of Jerusalem built a hospice and church here around 1190, giving the village its present name meaning 'hospice of John'. The hospice provided shelter and refreshment for those who passed by. The Knights became renowned for their hospitality, receiving privileges from both Welsh Princes and English kings, including the rights of sanctuary for their tenants and protection in Royal Courts. Cattle dealers travelled from far and wide to trade in the village's famous fairs, which were held seven times a year. After being destroyed by fire around 1400 during Owain Glyndŵr's rebellion against English rule it was rebuilt. Later it was taken over by outlaws who abused the rights of protection and became the scourge of the surrounding countryside. After years of lawlessness in the area, which included robbery, murder and cattle stealing, they were forced out in the early 16thC. In 1540 Henry VIII banned the Order of St John as part of his dissolution of monasteries and the hospice became a ruin.

The current Victorian St John's church was built where the hospice and original church once stood. Its graveyard contains graves of many dignitaries. Today the spirit of the Knights of St John lives on through the well known St John Ambulance Association. In 1700 almshouses were built for six 'poor aged men' from £200 bequeathed by Richard Vaughan. They were rebuilt in the 19thC.

YSBYTY IFAN TO PENMACHNO

12¾ or 3¾ miles

There are two alternative routes from Ysbyty Ifan to Penmachno.

Route A (12¾ miles) takes the longer and more challenging approach to Penmachno, but gives the satisfaction of following the infant river to its source at Llyn Conwy. The middle section crosses demanding and largely pathless Open Access land, rough underfoot. This route therefore is only suitable for experienced and well equipped hillwalkers who enjoy such a wild upland landscape. Given good weather and visibility this can be a magical and rewarding section of the trail. After sharing the initial climb from Ysbyty Ifan this route extends further along the upper Conwy valley by field paths and road, then follows a section of rough close river walking to waterfalls. It continues along a good track to Llyn Conwy, a large hidden upland lake lying nearly 1500 feet/460 metres amongst an expanse of remote blanket bog and heather moorland. After a choice of lakeside routes, a good path descends to a minor upland road which is followed down the dramatic side valley of Cwm Hafodyredwydd to the tiny community of Carrog. The route then continues along the lush Machno valley to Penmachno. If required the no. 64 bus can be taken from Carrog to Penmachno or Betws-y-Coed.

Route B (3¾ miles) in contrast will be the preferred choice for many people, as it follows the easier and more direct old drovers' route between the two communities, along which men once brought cattle from Anglesey to Mid-Wales. After climbing out of Ysbyty Ifan the route follows a scenic narrow upland road across attractive upland pasture above Cwm Eidda, then a track which rises steadily across rougher upland pasture to the bwlch (1280 feet/390 metres). The track now steadily descends the hillside, offering extensive views, then joins a minor road for the final descent to Penmachno.

Route A

10 Ysbyty Ifan to Ty Cipar

5¾ miles

The next section first rises by minor roads and track to the edge of open country, offering good mountain views. It then follows a path south-east across enclosed upland pasture, enjoying good views into the Vale of Conwy and to the Arenigs, before descending into the valley. After a section of unavoidable road walking the trail follows closely the river meandering along the wide reedy/tussocky valley at the edge of a wild remote upland area known as the Migneint. This last section is tough, but an opportunity for a final close encounter with the clear infant river, culminating in delightful waterfalls.

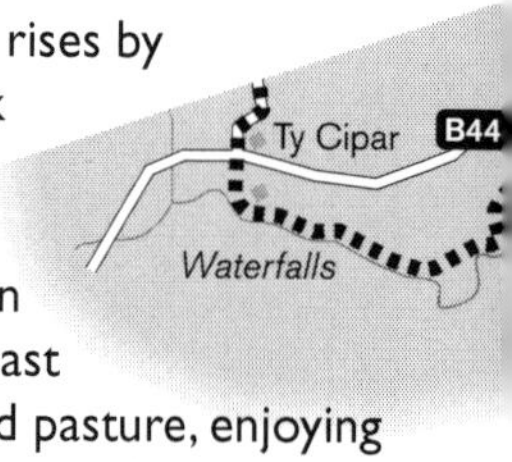

1 After visiting the village return to the B4407 and turn left past Ffynnon Penrhyn (1866), then right up a side road past the almshouses (see plaque). The road rises steadily. When it bends right to a house go up a stony tree-lined track ahead to a gate – *with good views across the valley.* Continue up the track to another gate and on up to a minor road. Turn right up the road, soon levelling out – *offering panoramic views towards Moel Siabod, the Glyders, Tryfan, the Carneddau mountains and north along the Conwy valley.* Go past the access track to Foel Gopyn, then follow a reedy stream left up to pass in front of the cottage and through a gate above. Go along the farm track across reedy upland pasture – *with a good view of the Arenigs and distant Arans.* When the track fades keep ahead to a stile and continue beneath the higher rocky slope to another stile. Go ahead past the top edge of a large reedy area. Ignore the higher path, but continue ahead across the mid-slopes down to a stile. Go ahead across the slope, later passing a small ruin then descending a track to a gate. Continue down to cross two streams then a stile. Descend the field to join a green track, which bends right by a stream. After a few yards go through a small gate on the left, then descend the field to a stile onto the B4407.

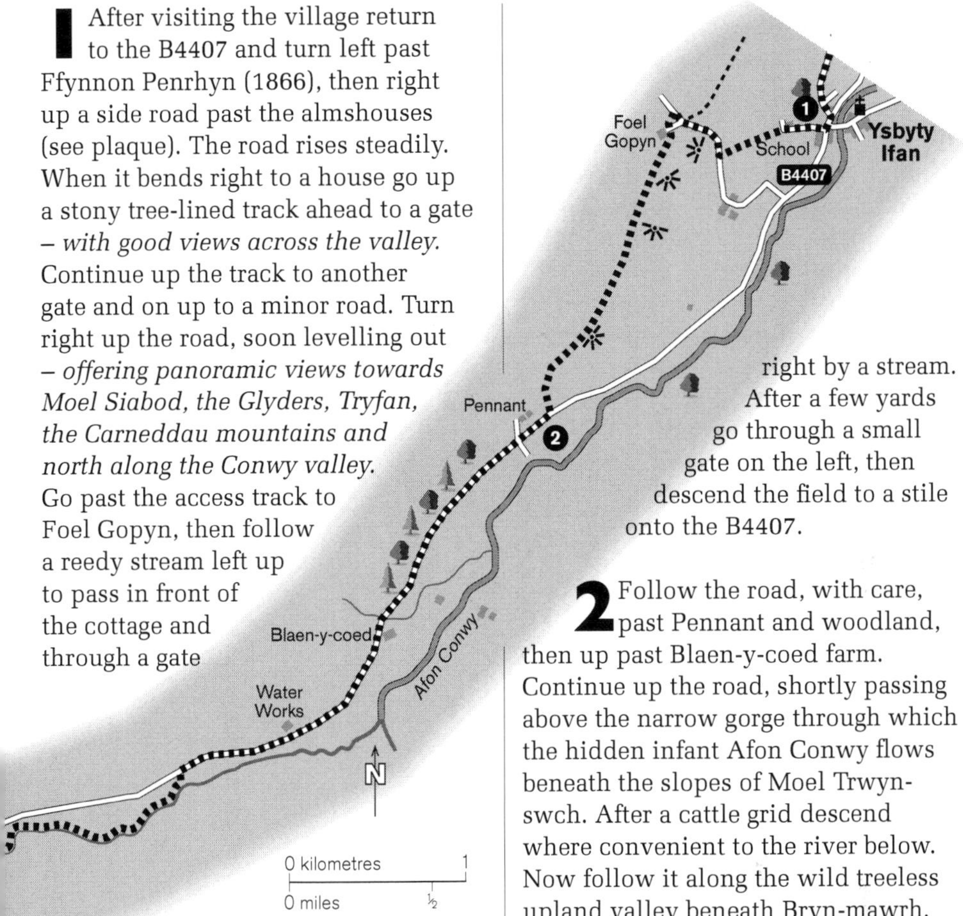

2 Follow the road, with care, past Pennant and woodland, then up past Blaen-y-coed farm. Continue up the road, shortly passing above the narrow gorge through which the hidden infant Afon Conwy flows beneath the slopes of Moel Trwyn-swch. After a cattle grid descend where convenient to the river below. Now follow it along the wild treeless upland valley beneath Bryn-mawrh. The terrain is reedy, tussocky, and wet in places, but you are rewarded with the intimacy of the delightful clear river so close to its source. Later you can continue more directly along the edge of higher ground overlooking the river. Eventually you climb up alongside a waterfall, then up past further stepped falls – *a great place to stop* – before heading away from the river up to the road by remote Ty Cipar. *This house was once used by Lord Penrhyn and his friends on fishing trips to nearby Llyn Conwy.*

11 Ty Cipar to Carrog

4½ or 4 miles

From Ty Cipar the trail follows a good track to Llyn Conwy, the generic source of the Afon Conwy, from which flows a strong feeder stream. You now work your way round either side of the lake on faint paths, with Route A being ½ mile longer but offering more views and passing an old boathouse and higher source feeder streams. Afterwards you follow a path west down to join a minor road, which makes a stunning descent through Cwm Hafodyredwydd to the tiny community of Carrog in the Machno valley.

1 Go through the gate adjoining Ty Cipar then follow the stony track north across the vast heather moorland – *enjoying a good view of Snowdon, the Glyders and Y Gamallt to the west.* The track crosses the feeder stream to the Conwy then a small solar powered building. Without warning the track ends at the edge of Llyn Conwy.

Llyn Conwy, a large natural lake now managed as a reservoir, lies amongst the expansive heather and blanket bog moorland of the Migneint, one the largest in Wales. When it was part of the Penrhyn Estate it was kept well stocked with fish for anglers. The boathouse by the outlet is still used today, and nearby is the small ruined dwelling used overnight by fishermen. On the north shore is another old boathouse. Whilst generally referred to as the source of the Conwy, there are short higher feeder streams which enter the lake along its northern shore, which perhaps technically better carry

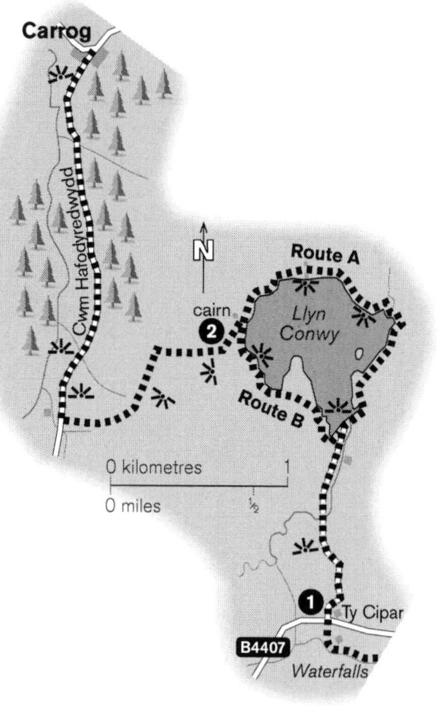

this status. In 1854 George Borrow passed this way whilst exploring North Wales on foot for his renowned guidebook 'Wild Wales'.

Route A: Cross the stream and keep ahead passing to the right of a wet area to cross a handrailed footbridge at the tip of the lake. Follow the path ahead, soon bending right and continuing a little way from the lake before returning to the shore opposite an island. After crossing two fences and a small footbridge continue near the rocky shore to the old boathouse. Now follow the path through heather to cross a ladder-stile, then along the edge of the lake and round its corner to an old waymark post below a stone cairn on higher ground.

Route B: Head back to the nearby ruined dwelling, then follow a faint path along the western edge of the lake, a few yards from the shore. After about 250 yards the path angles away from the lake and crosses high ground ahead, passing a small stone structure to your left. The faint path continues through the heather down to the lake then continues close along the lake's edge just above the water. Note the stone cairn on the skyline ahead. Shortly head up to a nearby old waymark post below the cairn to join a better path (Route A). Turn left.

2 The path rises gently across the heather slope, then heads away from the lake and continues west towards Y Gamallt – *with views of the Moelwyns, Cnicht, Snowdon, the Glyders and the Carneddau mountains.* The path, vague in places, then gently descends to a ladder-stile. Just beyond turn left and follow the path near the fence down to cross a small wet reedy area and a stream. The path briefly rises then just before a fence corner it bears right and continues near the fence, later descending to a minor road. Turn right past Hafodyredwydd and follow the road down the spectacular part wooded valley, later enjoying a good view down into Cwm Penmachno, with Moel Llechwedd Hafod dominating the valley ahead. After 1¾ miles you reach a junction at Carrog by cottages, telephone box and bus stop. (The road leading left goes along the valley to its end at the small slate quarrying community of Cwm Penmachno.)

12 Carrog to Penmachno

2½ miles

The trail now follows the Afon Machno, the first major tributary of the Afon Conwy, east along the attractive and lush valley grazed by sheep and cattle, using available field paths, to the small village of Penmachno.

1 Continue ahead along the road – *soon with a view east along the valley.* Just before the road bends across a stone bridge over the river, go through an iron gate on the right. Go along the field's right hand edge to a gate by a stream. Keep ahead across the large field to another gate, then follow a farm track towards Pen-y-bedw. After a gate go past outbuildings to another gate, past the house then go down its access track. After a cattle grid and a gate do not follow the track across the nearby bridge over the river, but turn right on a signposted path. Go along a wide initially reedy old green lane between boundaries to a gate above the river. Go along the walled track to go through another gate at sheep pens, then an adjoining small gate on the left. Turn right across a small fenced area to a nearby gate and continue across the slope to pass a wall corner beneath a telegraph pole, with a bridge over the river nearby.

2 Go along the raised edge of the next field soon joining a nearby farm track to go through a gate ahead. Follow the green track to another gate, then continue along the edge of a reedy stream to cross a large footbridge over a deep section of the river – *a great place to stop* – to a ladder-stile onto the road. Follow it right beneath Coed-Pen-y-bryn, soon passing the forest's entrance track at its corner. After a further 150 yards take a hedge-lined path angling down on the right, soon near the Afon Machno. After passing stepping stones the path moves away

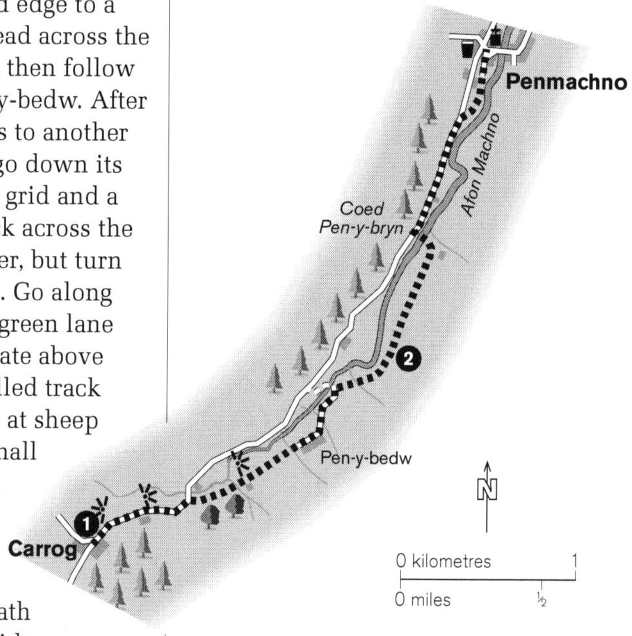

from the river to join a lane which continues past houses in Penmachno. When it splits take the narrow left fork to the road by The Eagles Inn.

Route B

13 Ysbyty Ifan to Penmachno

3¾ miles

1 After visiting the village return to the B4407. Turn left past Ffynnon Penrhyn (1866), then right up a side road past the almshouses. Shortly, when it bends right to a house go up a stony tree-lined track ahead to a gate – *with good views across the valley and further west the tops of the two Arenigs.* Continue up the track to another gate and on up to a minor road. Turn right up the road, soon levelling out – *offering panoramic views ahead to Moel Siabod, the Glyders, Tryfan, the Carneddau mountains and north along the Conwy valley.* Continue along the road past another road on the right, after which the narrow scenic upland road begins a long steady descent across upland pasture – *with views into Cwm Aidda.*

2 After crossing Pont Blaen-Eidda, when the road bends right, keep ahead up a rough track to cross Pont Rhyd-yr-halen to enter Open Access land. The track now rises steadily across reed and gorse-covered pasture to reach a ladder-stile/gate just below the top of the bwlch. The track soon begins a long steady descent – *enjoying views along the valley to the quarries at Cwm Penmachno and directly ahead to Moel Siabod* – to end at a gate near a house. Go down the wide stony access track which soon becomes a tarmaced road. It descends steadily, later passing a side road, to eventually reach the bend of the main road in Penmachno by the former Machno Inn. Follow the road left across the river to pass a bus shelter and nearby church to reach a junction at The Eagles Inn.

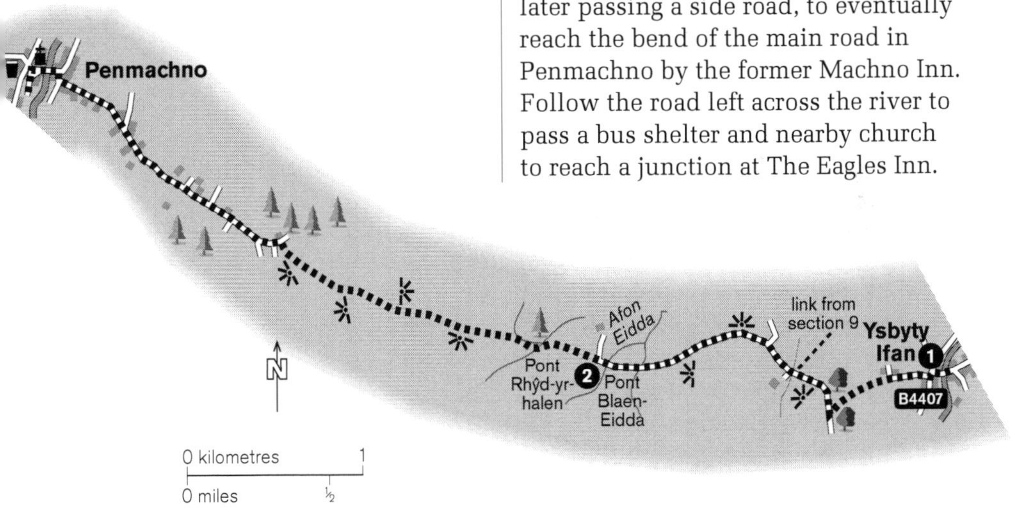

PENMACHNO TO BETWS-Y-COED

8 or 5½ miles

The next section of the trail heads back to Betws-y-Coed, later by a choice of higher or lower routes. On arrival at Betws-y-Coed you have the option of including the 1½ mile riverside walk from section 16 (paragraph 1) in this stage of the walk.

After following field paths along the Penmachno valley, the trail continues on forestry tracks through Coed Wern to visit the Roman Bridge, an ancient packhorse bridge. It then follows a scenic quiet country road past Machno Falls and Conwy gorge. **Route A** (8 miles) heads west along the wooded Lledr valley, then climbs through woodland to Llyn Elsi, an attractive popular upland reservoir lying about 755 feet/230 metres in part of Gwydyr Forest Park. It then does a near circuit of the lake following a waymarked white forest trail in reverse, before descending to Betws-y-Coed. **Route B** (5½ miles) continues down to cross the 15thC Pont-ar-Lledr, then incorporates a delightful, but optional, ¾ mile privately owned circular trail to the famous Fairy Glen, a deep narrow wooded section of the Conwy gorge, popular since Victorian times, before following a scenic road through woodland to Betws-y-Coed.

Formerly known as Pennant Machno this peaceful village, with its terraced stone houses, lies in the beautiful secluded Machno valley, only a short distance from Betws-y-Coed. A five-arched stone bridge built in 1785 over the river links both parts of the community. The parish church of St Tudclud built in 1857 where once stood two churches, contains several inscribed late 5thC/ mid 6thC stones. These are evidence of early Christianity in the area.

14 Penmachno to Betws-y-Coed (section 1)

3 miles

1 From The Eagles Inn take the side road signposted to Ty Mawr. Almost immediately turn right and follow the road past the imposing chapel, a utility area and on over the river. At the end of Ty'n-y ddol turn right along a track to a facing gate. Here go through a small wooden gate on the left and continue along the field edge to a kissing gate. Follow the green access track to pass through an old farm to a ladder-stile. Keep ahead across two fields to a ladder-stile and footbridge, then continue across the next large field. Go past a facing gate by two barns, then turn left to a stile. Go up the stony track then just before a cattle grid take a waymarked path through a gate on the right. Go along the bottom field edge and through a gateway. Continue through the next field, over a stream then near the river. Just before a facing gate ahead angle left to cross an old wall and a stile

beyond. Continue between the wood perimeter fence and a wall, then just before you reach the a gateway in the wall ahead, cross a stile on the left to join a forestry track above. Follow it right along the open edge of the forest, later becoming enclosed by trees.

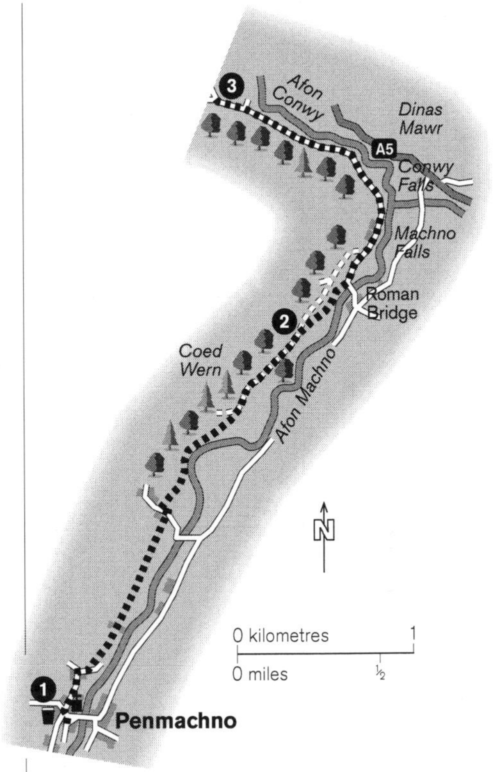

2 After a further 100 yards, just before the track rises and bends left, look for a stile down to your right, adjoining another. (Alternatively continue up the forestry track, soon joining another which then steadily descends. Just after it bends left descend right through the trees to a minor road below.) After crossing the stile follow a path left beside the fence along the wood edge to another stile. Continue with the path through woodland, soon near the river and rising to a good view across to the former woollen mill, after which it descends to a minor road. First turn right to the bridge over the Afon Penmachno by the former Penmachno Woollen Mill – *built originally in the 1830s as a water powered fulling mill. Just downstream is the ancient packhorse bridge, known as 'Roman Bridge'.* Return along the road and follow it to Pandy Mill, opposite which a path leads past the ruined corn mill to Machno Falls. Continue along the road, past a viewpoint of the Conwy gorge and later with Dinas Mawr towering above the valley. *Dinas Mawr greatly impressed George Borrow, which he described as 'an immense mountain' in his famous book 'Wild Wales', when he walked beneath it in 1854.* Later you pass a row of terraced cottages. Just beyond the road descends to a forestry track and minor road on the left. Here you have a choice.

15 Penmachno to Betws-y-Coed (section 2)

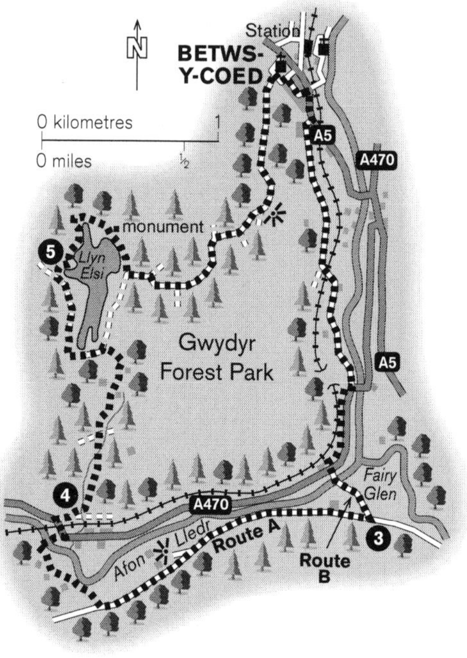

Route A

5 miles

3 Turn left along the road signposted to Ty Mawr. The attractive narrow road heads west past two houses and along the wooded Lledr valley, shortly briefly above the tree-lined river. After passing terraced cottages the road begins to rise steadily and passing the entrance to Ty'n y Berth – *with a good view across the wooded Lledr valley and to Moel Siabod.* (A nearby riverside path becomes rough underfoot and overgrown later, hence the preference to staying on this delightful narrow road.) Shortly the road levels out with a waymarked path on the left. Here take a path angling right off the road beside a wall down through trees, soon sunken in character, to a ladder-stile/bridle gate. Continue down the wide tree-lined path and on above the river. After crossing a small stone bridge over a side stream continue along the old walled green track. When it bends left towards a nearby cottage, turn right through an old gateway. Follow the path to cross a large footbridge over the river, then continue through trees to the A470. Cross the road and follow it left to pass with care under nearby Pont Gethin – *a railway viaduct built in 1875-78 by Gethin, a local builder* – then turn right along the access track leading to Craig Lledr.

4 After about 40 yards, take a signposted path on the left. It angles up through the trees, crosses a footbridge, then rises steeply up the wooded slope near the stream, later becoming less steep and crossing the stream. At a forestry track, take a level path almost opposite through the trees. Shortly it rises to a small ruin, then continues up through the wood, soon being joined by a less distinct path coming in from another ruin to your left. Beyond a stream the path rises left then levels out and continues beside a short section of wall and through trees up to emerge on a stony forestry track by hidden Llyn Elsi. Follow it left, shortly descending to a left-hand bend. Here, go past a waymark post on the right and up the white trail stony path. Follow the undulating trail path, soon heading north. After crossing a turning area continue along a forestry track.

Shortly the track bends west towards Moel Siabod, where it overlooks a narrow arm of the lake.

5 Here, at a waymark post go down the stony trail path on the right to a footbridge and continue near the water's edge to a prominent viewpoint across the lake – *a good place to stop to watch the various wildfowl and dragonflies.* The path now meanders round the western side of the lake to the dam. Here turn left up steps, and follow the path down to a footbridge over the lake's outlet to reach a path junction below the dam. Keep ahead and follow the stony path up to a monument and seats – *offering a great view south along the lake and mountain views from Moel Siabod to the Carneddau range. The monument was erected to commemorate the opening of the Betws-y-Coed waterworks in 1914, when the lake became a reservoir providing water for the town.* Follow the waymarked stony path down towards the lake and on along its eastern edge, then turn left along the stony forestry track on the waymarked white trail. At the track junction turn right, then at the next take the left fork. Follow the forestry track through the mature trees, bearing right at the next junction, soon beginning a long steady descent and being joined by a blue trail to eventually leave Gwydyr Forest Park to reach the road behind St Mary's church in Betws-y-Coed. Follow it right past Church Hill House, then take a side road on the right, soon bending left down to the main road. Cross to Ffordd Hen Eglwys opposite.

Route B

2½ miles

3 Continue down the road to cross the 15thC Pont-ar-Lledr to reach the A470. Cross the road and follow a roadside walkway right to a side road at Beaver Bridge – *named after the still river below the bridge known as the 'beavers pool'.* To visit Fairy Glen cross the bridge with care then go up a track signposted to Fairy Glen/Cymanog Isaf Farm by nearby Fairy Glen Hotel. After passing a car park you reach a small gate on the right marking the start of a delightful ¾ mile circular trail to the Fairy Glen, with a nominal charge payable. Follow the gravel path to a path junction, turn left and follow it to another path junction above the river. Follow the path left to the entrance of Fairy Glen. Return to the path junction and continue on the riverside walk past the confluence of the Lledr and Conwy rivers, and on back to the entrance. Retrace your steps to cross Beaver Bridge, then turn right along the side road. This scenic road initially runs near the river, then passes under the railway line and continues through attractive mature woodland to reach the main road in Betws-y-Coed by Cotswold Outdoor shop after ¾ mile. Turn left past the newsagents, then take the first road on the right (Ffordd Hen Eglwys) signposted to the Railway Museum/golf course.

BETWS-Y-COED TO TREFRIW

12¾, 11¼ or 8¼ miles

16 Betws-y-Coed to Llyn Parc

3¼ miles

After a delightful section of riverside walking to the confluence of the Llugwy and Conwy rivers the trail returns to the centre of Betws-y-Coed, then enters nearby Gwydyr Forest Park, an upland area that once supported a thriving lead-mining industry. It follows waymarked forest trails up past a good viewpoint overlooking Betws-y-Coed to the end of Llyn Parc, a large attractive lake lying at an altitude of about 656 feet/200 metres, hidden in the forest.

1 Go along Ffordd Hen Eglwys, over the railway line and on to reach St Michael's church by the suspension bridge. *This 14thC church, occupying the site of an ancient religious house, served as the parish church until the larger St Mary's was built to accommodate the religious needs of 19thC tourists.* After visiting the church follow a path through the churchyard above the river, then continue along the road to the entrance to the golf club. Keep ahead along the waymarked riverside path to a kissing gate, then around the edge of the golf course to a kissing gate and a seat at the confluence of the Llugwy and Conwy rivers. After another kissing gate the path continues along the edge of the golf course, passes under a railway bridge and continues past Royal Oak Farm Cottage to a gate by

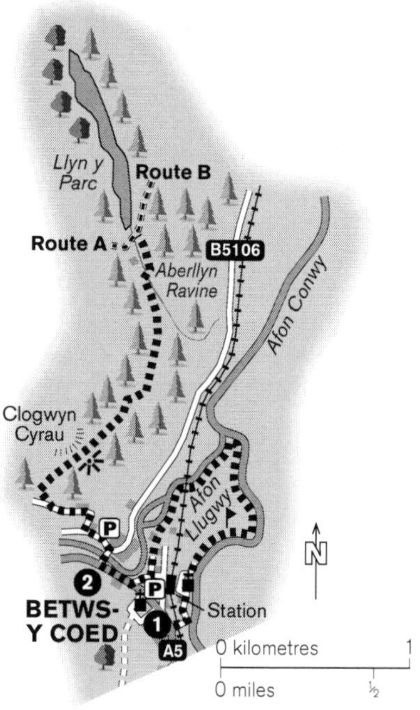

the Snowdonia National Park offices and Tourist Information Centre. Bear right along the roadway signposted to Pont-y-Pair bridge to reach the main road by the Royal Oak Hotel. Turn right along the pavement past guest houses and shops.

2 Shortly turn right on the B5106 across Pont-y-Pair over the river. *Pont-y-Pair (Bridge of the Cauldron) is said to have been built across the Afon Llugwy during the 15thC by a mason called Howel, who died before its completion.* At the far side turn left along a minor road past a car park and toilets. Continue up the single track road, then turn right up a no through

Llyn Parc

road on the waymarked forest trails. Shortly the road bends left up past wooden houses and becomes a stony track as it enters the forest. Take the waymarked blue and white forest trails on the right into the trees. At the waymarked path junction turn right [Cyrau]. Follow the waymarked white trail up through the trees, soon passing beneath the crag of Clogwyn Cyrau and descending to a viewpoint overlooking Betws-y-Coed. Keep away from the cliff edge. The undulating path continues through mixed woodland, later descending to a crossroad of paths. Turn left up the waymarked yellow trail. The path rises steadily, then crosses a part open steep wooded slope, before rising up the edge of the narrowing Aberllyn Ravine above the stream to reach the top of a small waterfall. *The sealed mine entrances, debris and ruins are relics of lead and zinc mines that were worked here during the 18thC until their abandonment early last century.* After crossing a footbridge over the stream, go along the forest edge past a nearby cottage and continue along a narrow track to reach a stony forestry track with a seat ahead at the end of Llyn Parc. *The water level of this sheltered remote lake is now much lower than when it provided water power for the mines. Today, despite its life-restricting high-level mineral content, it is a tranquil place to have a break.*

17 Llyn Parc to Trefriw

From Llyn Parc you have a choice of interesting routes to Trefriw.

Route A (9½ or 8 miles) takes a longer, meandering, more demanding undulating approach through Gwydyr Forest Park, full of interest, to the forest's northern edge where it meets the foothills of the Carneddau. It features several other scenic upland lakes that once provided water for the lead-mines, a visit to Conwy valley's most beautiful and popular large lakes, and extensive mountain views. The stunning scenery makes this route one of the highlights of the trail.

At first it follows a waymarked trail through the forest, then heads north up a forestry track to Llyn Sarnau and the nearby 19thC Llanrwst lead mine engine-house. The route then follows another waymarked forest trail in reverse to delightful little known upland lakes at just over 1000 feet, before leaving it to pass Llyn Glangors. After crossing upland pasture it descends to Llyn Geirionydd, then continues alongside the lake to its end. Here you have the option of following an attractive alternative described route, 1½ miles shorter, along the western side of Llyn Geirionydd. Otherwise the main route follows a waymarked trail on a short climb up across the forested ridge of Mynydd Deulyn, reaching a height of just under 1000 feet/300 metres, and down to the adjoining valley where lies Llyn Crafnant – one of Snowdonia's hidden gems. It then follows a narrow road along the southern side of Llyn Crafnant, past a lakeside seasonal café which may tempt you to linger in this beautiful spot. Later it climbs back over the part-wooded hillside past an old mine site on another waymarked trail to a monument at the end of Llyn Geirionydd, where you are joined by the alternative route. From here you follow the wooded edge of Cwm Crafnant down to Trefriw.

Route B (5 miles) continues more directly to Trefriw via Llanrwst midway, featuring easier forest and riverside walking, and an option to visit Gwydir Castle, said to be one of the most haunted houses in Wales (01492 641687/ www.gwydircastle.co.uk). The route first follows a waymarked forest trail along the eastern edge of Gwydyr Forest Park, descending in stages to the valley, where it follows the Afon Conwy to Pont Fawr at Llanrwst. It continues on track and field paths to rejoin the Afon Conwy, later following the Afon Crafnant to Trefriw.

Route A

9½ or 8 miles

1 Turn left and follow the stony track up through the forest. Go past a path on the left then a waymarked path on the right (an alternative short cut but boggy in parts) – *soon with a good view of Moel Siabod.* At a forestry track junction turn right. Shortly, follow the waymarked blue trail/path left up through trees, soon descending. Take the waymarked trail left fork to a stile at the wood edge, then follow the blue trail between two stone barns and along a green track to pass in front of Coed Mawr to cross a ladder-stile. Follow the trail path across the meadow – *with a view now of Tryfan and the Carneddau*

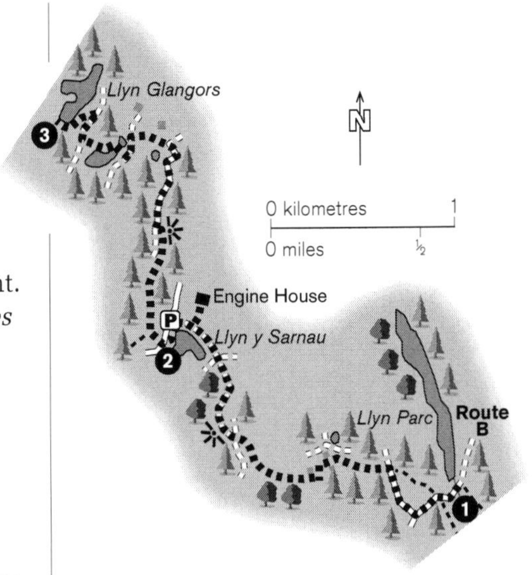

mountains – to cross a stile, then follow the enclosed path to a ladder-stile. Here ignore the descending blue trail and cross a stile on the right, then go across a delightful traditional meadow to a ladder-stile near the corner onto a stony forestry track. Go up the track, soon joined by another at a great viewpoint. *The panorama of mountains includes Moel Siabod, Snowdon, the Glyders and Tryfan.* Continue up the stony track, shortly levelling out. At a crossroad of tracks keep ahead, soon passing Llyn Sarnau ('lake of the old tracks'). Shortly turn sharp right up another forestry track to cross the second ladder-stile on the left. Follow the signposted path to the impressive stone chimney of the Llanrwst lead-mine engine house – *built in 1876/77 to pump water from the mine.* Follow the waymarked path above Nant B. H. Outdoor Centre to a path junction. Bear right, then left down to a ladder-stile to rejoin the main forestry track. Follow it right to a road then turn left along the edge of Llyn Sarnau car park to an information board.

2 Cross the road to the start of the Forest Lakes Walk opposite and angle right up into the wood on the yellow trail. After 40 yards when the waymarked yellow trail turns left keep ahead. You are now going to follow the yellow trail in reverse to near Llyn Glangors. The path rises steadily in stages through the wood. At a path junction bear right on the waymarked path, briefly descending then continuing through mature woodland. At a waymark post keep ahead a few yards to the signed viewpoint looking down the wooded valley towards Llanrwst. Keep away from the edge. Return to the waymark post and follow the trail path right to the nearby forestry track. Follow it right. After several bends, the yellow trail turns left off the track up through a clearing scarred by mining, then continues to another forestry track. Follow it left past a small attractive lake, then at a waymark post turn right down the trail path and on between the first lake and a larger one – *with a good view to the Glyders and Tryfan. These attractive lily-covered lakes, known as the Three Dams Reservoir, are a great place to stop to watch the dragonflies.* The path continues along the larger lake's northern side and on through trees to reach a forestry track. Turn right – *soon enjoying a view of Llyn Glangors.* Go past where the yellow trail descends on the left. About 75 yards further along the track do a sharp U-turn left down a signed path to a ladder-stile near Llyn Glangors.

3 Go across the end of the lake to a stile and up to a telegraph pole on a small rise. Continue down the slope, past another telegraph pole, to a ladder-stile. Follow the path through reeds and on to pass a further telegraph pole – *with a good view of Moel Siabod* – then descend to another ladder-stile. Continue to a track by the lower of two concrete buildings on the site of the former New Pandora lead mine. Turn right up the track, then at the second building, turn left across the old mine to go through a gate in the fence on your right. Continue to a nearby ladder-stile, then follow the path across the part heather covered terrain – *soon with the sight of Llyn Geirionydd below.* The path makes a long steady descent to the lakeside road. *Almost 1 mile long Llyn Geirionydd is the only lake in Snowdonia where powerboats and water skiing are permitted. This beautiful upland lake once echoed to the sound of intensive mining in the 1870s. From the Pandora mine at the southern end of Llyn Geirionydd lead and zinc ore were carried by a tramway along the eastern side of the lake, then lowered by an aerial cableway for processing at Klondyke Mill in the valley below. Trees were planted here in 1929 to soften the scarred landscape.* (If for any reason you need to shorten the walk simply follow the lakeside road north to point 6.) Follow the road left along the eastern side of the lake, past a slipway and car park/toilets – *built on the waste tip of part of the Pandora mine complex, which eventually closed in 1906* – then turn right on a waymarked blue trail along a forestry track past the end of the lake.

4 On its bend you have a choice:

Alternative route

For the shorter alternative cross a stile by a gate on the right. Follow the path beneath the cottage and on to the edge of Llyn Geirionydd and a stile at the wood corner. The path keeps close to the wooded edge of the lake, later climbing a small rocky spur above a corner of the lake, before descending near a fence enclosing an old mine to continue along the lakeside. After a stile keep ahead then follow a waymarked path angling right alongside a low wall to reach a track beyond a stone building. After visiting the nearby monument follow the track to join the valley road at point 6.

Main route

For Llyn Crafnant continue up the stony forestry track on the waymarked blue trail beneath woodland. You can simply stay with the blue trail as it follows the meandering forestry track up the hillside or short cut it by following sections of a path as follows. At a trail waymark post just before a bend turn right up a short path through the trees to rejoin the track. As the path opposite can be muddy follow the track right, soon bending left. At the cross-path by a blue trail waymark post

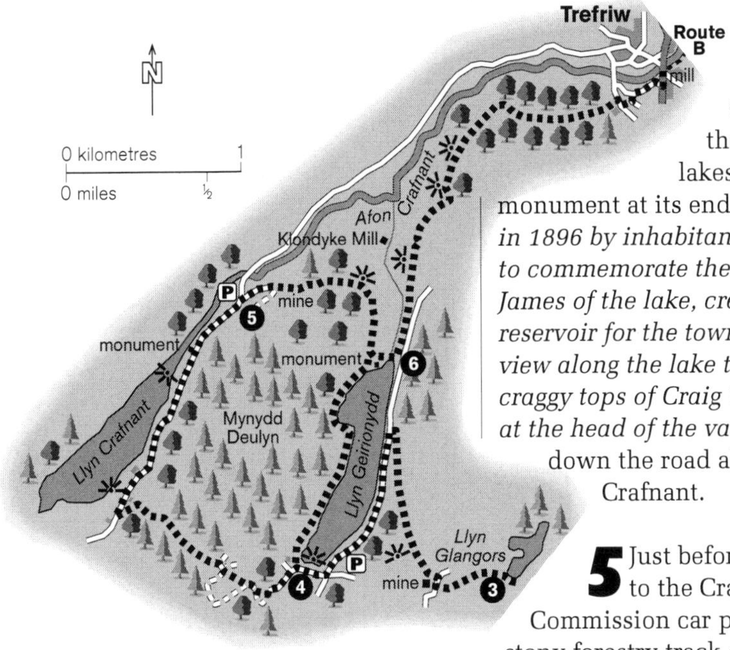

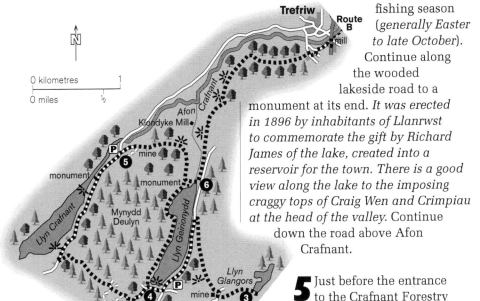

and a stream turn right and follow the path up through trees to rejoin the blue trail near the bend of the forestry track. Continue up the track and when it bends right follow the waymarked blue trail up the wooded slope ahead. After passing through a wall gap the blue trail continues through conifers, soon descending in stages. At a ladder-stile – *with your first view of Llyn Crafnant* – turn sharp left down the blue trail to reach a minor road by a small derelict stone building, a former chapel. Turn right past a nearby telephone box and follow this scenic narrow valley road enjoying a good view over the lake. *Llyn Crafnant, ¾ mile long, means 'lake in the valley of garlic'. It contains rainbow and wild brown trout, making it popular with fishermen.* Shortly you pass Cynllwyd Mawr, which has a café and lakeside tea gardens during the fishing season (*generally Easter to late October*). Continue along the wooded lakeside road to a monument at its end. *It was erected in 1896 by inhabitants of Llanrwst to commemorate the gift by Richard James of the lake, created into a reservoir for the town. There is a good view along the lake to the imposing craggy tops of Craig Wen and Crimpiau at the head of the valley.* Continue down the road above Afon Crafnant.

5 Just before the entrance to the Crafnant Forestry Commission car park go up a wide stony forestry track on the right on a waymarked Trefriw Trails 5 and red forest trail. When it does a sharp U-turn right, keep ahead on the Trefriw Trail across a turning area and up to a stile. The path then rises to the remains of a slate mine, with its stone buildings, mine entrances and spoil heaps. *Slate was extracted from the hillside here from the 18thC until the early 20thC.* Continue on the path across the part tree and bracken covered hillside, shortly descending to a Trefriw Trails 5 waymark post at a path junction. Go down the left fork to a wall gap and on with the undulating path, shortly bending right to cross a ladder-stile. Go up the stony path, through an old wall, then pass to the left of conifers and continue along a wide level green path. Soon angle left up to the nearby monument offering a good view along Llyn Geirionydd.

The monument was erected in 1850 to commemorate the reputed birthplace of Talisien, a 6thC chief bard. It was toppled in a 1976 storm, then re-erected in 1994. In summer, parties of Victorian visitors came here, often entertained by music and sports. Between 1863-1922, an annual poetry/musical event, first established by local poet Gwilym Cowlyd, was held at the monument. Descend to the part stony track below and follow it left across the outlet of the lake to a kissing gate onto the lakeside road. Turn left.

6 Continue with a path by the fence parallel with the road and the nearby river to a ladder-stile. Follow the path to another ladder-stile and continue along the former tramway to a seat and an information board at a good viewpoint overlooking wooded Cwm Crafnant. *Visible in the valley below is Klondyke Mill (1900-11), which was powered by water from the Afon Geirionydd.* The path now passes through a tiny side valley to a small wooden gate, then continues across the steep wooded slope, before descending past a good viewpoint. After crossing the part wooded slope above Cwm Crafnant, it descends through deciduous woodland to a stile, then continues down to a road at the outskirts of Trefriw. Turn right up the road, then just beyond Y Wern take a signposted enclosed path angling back on the left down to join a road, which you follow down to a junction. Turn right and follow the road down to the B5106 by the school. Turn left to reach nearby Trefriw Woollen Mill.

Route B

5 miles

1 Turn right along the stony forestry track shared with a mountain bike trail. Just after the track bends left, where it meets other narrow tracks, turn right on the waymarked yellow trail. Follow the green/stony track through the open forest, shortly

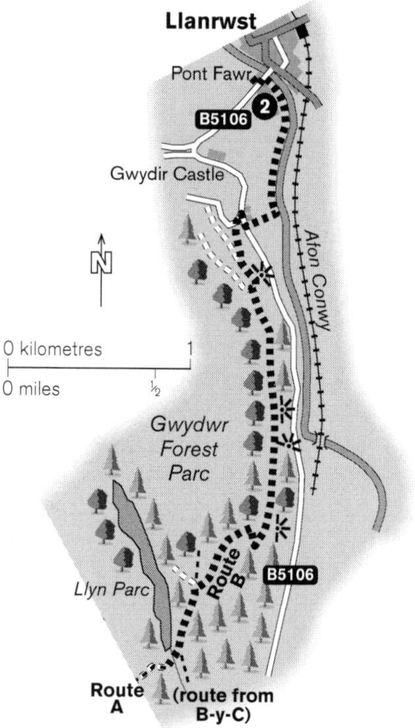

bending right and descending. Soon it becomes a stony path which bends right down the wooded slope, then does a sharp U-turn and continues down and across the part wooded slope – *offering good views into the Conwy valley, and ahead to Llanrwst.* Shortly it becomes a narrow stony track, later gently descending through trees. When it meets another track, follow the yellow trail down its right fork past the nearby picnic area – *offering good views down to the river and to Llanrwst.* At a waymark post turn right on a waymarked public path. Follow the initially stony path down through the forest to the bend of a road, which you follow down to the B5106. *Nearby Gwydir Castle, dating from the 16thC, was the seat of the influential Wynn family. The house is said to be one of the most haunted in Wales.* Cross the road and turn right along the grass verge. Shortly cross a ladder-stile and go down the field edge, to cross a stile near the river. Walk along the river bank towards Llanrwst to reach the road at Pont Fawr, with Tuhwnt i'r Bont tea-rooms opposite.

2 Just beyond Tuhwnt i'r Bont follow a signposted path along a hedge-lined track on the right. After ⅓ mile as it bends left, cross a ladder-stile on the right. Follow the stiled path along the edge of four fields. After passing over a water course cross a stile just beyond and continue along the embanked path to another stile at the end of a large suspension bridge over the Afon Conwy. *This is a mid-20thC replacement for the original wooden Gower's Bridge, named after the Rev. John Gower, who also*

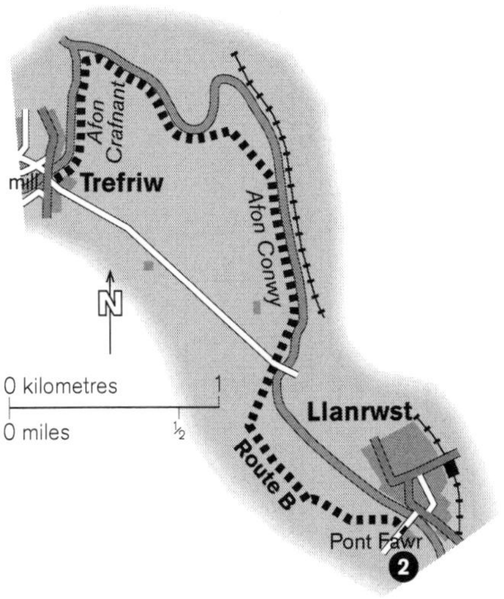

built the lane ahead in the 1880s to provide a link, financed by tolls levied, between Trefriw and Llanrwst railway station. Horse-drawn carriages would take visitors to sample the water at Trefriw Spa. Fishing was popular with Victorian visitors, and coracles were a common sight on the river. Cross the stile opposite and follow the riverside path along the top of the flood embankment, through kissing gates, later leaving the Afon Conwy and heading south alongside the Afon Crafnant towards Trefriw. Go past a footbridge, through a kissing gate and briefly along a track, before following an enclosed riverside path to toilets and a road junction beyond. Cross the main road to Trefriw woollen mill.

TREFRIW TO PONTWGAN

9 or 8 miles

From Trefriw the trail continues north to Dolgarrog via woodland, upland pasture and the steep wooded slopes of Coed Dolgarrog National Nature Reserve, offering a choice of routes, with Route A providing a fascinating insight into the upland landscape's industrial history. It then continues on a lower less demanding route to the hamlet of Pontwgan, near Rowen.

Trefriw, standing on Sarn Helen, a major Roman Road beneath the wooded western slopes of the Conwy valley was once an important inland port serving the valley and nearby Llanrwst, the tidal limit of the river. In the first half of the 19thC, vessels up to 100 tons carried coal, lime, wine and general goods up the river, and returned to the coast full of slate, grain, wool, lead ore and timber from the surrounding hills. Up to 450 boats traded from the quay to places such as Liverpool and Dublin. Trade peaked in 1862 after which it declined due to the arrival of the railway in the valley during that decade. Trefriw also had a small boatyard and became an important cloth-weaving centre. A fulling mill, taking woven cloth from cottages to wash and finish, was established in 1820. It then developed into the existing woollen mill, one of the finest surviving tweed mills in Wales. Its traditional Welsh goods are as popular today as in Victorian/Edwardian times when Trefriw became a fashionable spa resort. The curative properties of the sulphur and iron-rich waters of the chalybeate wells, to the north of the village and known since Roman times, attracted many visitors.

From 1847 until World War II passenger paddle steamer services to Trefriw developed, at their peak bringing up to 1000 people a day along the river from Conwy, Llandudno and Deganwy. These services were dependent on regular dredging of the river. More visitors arrived by train at nearby Llanrwst and Trefriw station. The village's heyday for visitors was in the early 20thC, but it still remains popular today and is a good starting point for walks. Of various industries once dependent on the river Crafnant, including a cornmill, sawmill, and forge which made hammers/chisels for the slate quarries, only the woollen mill survives, with power provided by hydro-electric turbines.

18 Trefriw to Dolgarrog

5¾ or 4¾ miles

The route first passes Fairy Falls then follows a waymarked woodland trail around Coed Creigiau above Trefriw, before joining a scenic upland road, reaching a height of 886 feet/270 metres. It then follows a path down to cross the Afon Ddu in a section of Coed Dolgarrog National Nature Reserve.

Soon afterwards you have a choice of routes. **Route A** (4¾ miles) climbs steadily across open country to cross a leat to join a hillside pipeline from Llyn Cowlyd at a height of 1083 feet/330 metres, offering extensive views. The route then follows pipelines down to Dolgarrog, on a steep descent, featuring a zig-zag path through mature woodland of Coed Dolgarrog National Nature Reserve. **Route B** (5¾ miles) makes an earlier descent through Coed Dolgarrog National Nature Reserve, then extends alongside the Afon Ddu to a bridge over the Afon Conwy, before returning through woodland to Dolgarrog.

1 From the woollen mill follow the pavement across the bridge over the river past shops and a café, then turn left up the side road. After 15 yards, take a signposted path on the left, soon above the river. Go past a footbridge and through a kissing gate, then continue under a high footbridge to reach a seat at Fairy Falls. *The name reflects the fascination Victorians had with fairies. In summer the falls are a mere trickle as water is diverted through a large pipe opposite to create electricity for the woollen mill below.* Follow the path up to a kissing gate at the end of the footbridge, then the enclosed path ahead to a road. Turn left up the road then at a junction turn right. At crossroads turn left up the road, then go up a road on the right signposted to the cemetery and Llyn Cowlyd. Just past Ty-Creigiau turn right up a track on a waymarked 'Trefriw Trails 6' path into Coed Creigiau, an area of mixed woodland. When it splits take the waymarked right fork. After passing a good viewpoint looking down to the river Conwy, the waymarked trail turns left off the track and rises steadily through conifers, soon following a cross-path right up to a stony forestry track. Follow it right up to a track junction. Here turn left up the other track, then after about 150 yards follow a green track angling left off the stony forestry track to reach a seat at a good viewpoint looking across the Conwy valley to Llanrwst. About 100 yards further take a wide path on the right up to rejoin the forestry track. Follow it left, soon descending to leave Coed Creigiau to rejoin the minor road left earlier. *Ahead is a good view along Cwm Crafnant to Klondyke mill.* Continue up the attractive narrow road.

2 At a junction turn right on waymarked Trail 9. Continue along this delightful scenic upland road, later enjoying extensive views along the Conwy valley. The road then rises in stages, later passing two houses – *and providing new views west across wild upland pasture to the Carneddau mountain range and north to the Conwy estuary, the Ormes, and Conwy Mountain.* On the hillside ahead is a large black pipeline which Route A will join. *The pipeline brings water from Llyn Cowlyd tor the hydro-electric power station at Dolgarrog.* Shortly the road descends to a large modern house at another good viewpoint. Continue down the road. Just before farm buildings cross a ladder-stile on the right. Go down the field edge to a ladder-stile in the bottom corner. Just beyond turn right down to another ladder-stile into woodland. After passing to the right of a gully and stream work your way down the steep wooded slope to cross an iron girder footbridge over the Afon Ddu. A sign welcomes you to Coed Dolgarrog National Nature Reserve. *The Reserve, which is managed by the Countryside Council for Wales, contains two distinct types of woodland: rare wet elder along the banks of the Afon Ddu and semi-natural broad-leaved beech woodland.* Follow the waymarked path right through the trees, full of bluebells in May. At another post the path angles left up to a ladder-stile into a field. Angle left up to a waymark post. Here you have a choice.

Route A

3 Continue up the field to a ladder-stile by gates in the top right hand corner. Head up the middle of the large field to a gate in the corner onto an embankment above a leat. Go along the embankment to cross a footbridge over the leat. Head directly up the hillside, over a green, then a stony track to reach a level green track. *This is a former narrow gauge tramway built in 1916/17 to Llyn Cowlyd to facilitate work on building a higher dam to increase the lake's capacity in providing water via the existing pipeline to generate hydro-electric power for the aluminium works at Dolgarrog. The tramway closed in 1968.* Go through a set of gates in the fence and angle right up a faint green track to join the large pipeline above. *Little now remains of the medieval*

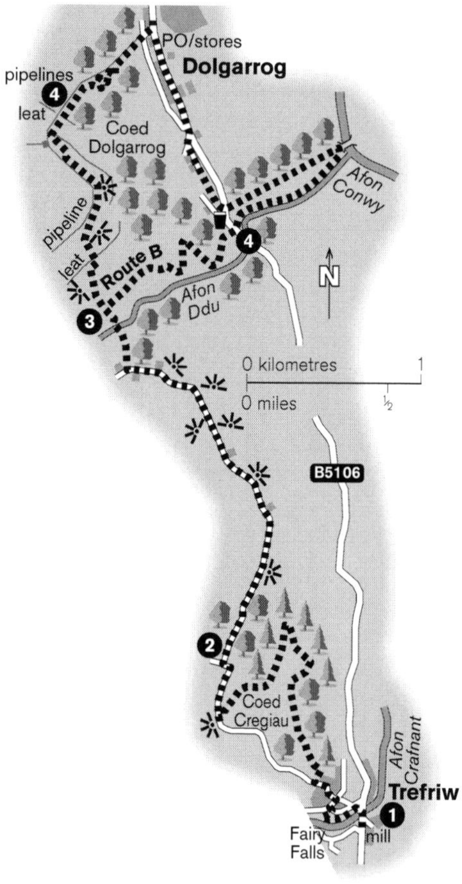

township of Ardda, the agricultural community which occupied this upland area as late as the 18thC. Continue beside it – *soon with a view of an old leat below* – shortly bending left to a stile – *enjoying great views of the meandering river Conwy, the Ormes, and Tal-y-fan.* Continue along the pipeline to another stile by point 506, then angle down through the trees to join a green track below. Follow it to cross the old leat to go through a gate. Turn left along the rough track. After 20 yards turn right to descend beside the old concrete supports of a pipeline parallel with a nearby complete pipeline to a stony track. *This is the Cowlyd tramway. Just beyond the pipelines near a corrugated former loco shed it connected with an earlier tramway built for the building of a dam at Llyn Eigiau. The Eigiau tramway largely followed the line of another tramway built in 1861-63 to transport slate from remote upland Cedryn and Cwm Eigiau quarries to here at the top of the Dolgarrog escarpment, from where it descended inclines to the valley and taken to Trefriw quay. Later the inclines were used to haul up steam engines by cables to reach the Eigiau and Cowlyd tramways. The one that you will now descend was later utilised to support large pipes carrying water rom both Cowlyd and Coedty reservoirs down to the hydro-electric power station at Dolgarrog aluminium works.*

4 Cross a small gated footbridge over the leat ahead, then descend a path between the pipeline and the wood perimeter fence to a stile below a building through which runs the adjoining pipeline, at an intersection of pipes. Turn right down to another stile to re-enter Coed Dolgarrog National Nature Reserve. Now slowly and with care follow the zig zag path down the steep wooded slope of the mature deciduous woodland, later passing the fenced edge of a quarry. At a path junction, take the left fork to a nearby stile, then follow the path down beside the pipeline to a kissing gate onto a road. Turn left over the pipeline then right down a fenced path to reach the main road in Dolgarrog, with the post office, stores and bus stop along to the right.

Route B

3 Turn right to cross a ladder-stile in the wall. Keep ahead passing to the right of a small waterworks station and follow the waymarked path through trees. After a stream angle right down to another stream and to a ladder-stile beyond. Go along the bottom field edge to another ladder-stile. Keep ahead to a waymark post, then continue down beside the fence on your right. At another post the path leaves the fence and continues down to a track. Follow it down to a ladder-stile/gate to re-enter Coed Dolgarrog National Nature Reserve by water treatment works. Continue down the increasingly steep concrete access lane, later passing an information board at a cattle grid to eventually reach the B5106 by Pont Dolgarrog. (If time is pressing turn left to reach the nearby Lord Newborough pub/bus stop and signposted path beyond.)

4 Cross the road to the entrance to a parking area and follow a path straight ahead through trees, soon above the river to a stile. Continue along the embanked riverside path to a ladder-stile then across open reedy terrain to eventually cross a stile by a girder bridge carrying water mains pipes over the river Conwy. *Between 1916-60 this bridge once provided a rail link for transporting goods from Dolgarrog aluminium works to the Conwy Valley line on the opposite*

Water pipeline above Coed Dolgarrog

side of the river. Prior to this the works were serviced by boats on the river taking goods to first Conwy, then a quay at Llandudno Junction. Turn left through the trees to a stile/gate and go along a track. After about 100 yards at telegraph pole D15, angle left and follow the right fork of a path/green track through trees to eventually reach the B5106 near the Lord Newborough pub. Take a signposted path opposite up through trees to a ladder-stile, then across the wooded slope to a kissing gate/gate. Continue along Bibby Road past houses then down to the main road. Continue along the pavement through Dolgarrog to reach the post office and stores.

Dolgarrog was regarded as the industrial heart of the Conwy valley with an interesting industrial history utilising available water power. An 18thC flour mill on the Afon Porthlwyd later became a paper mill. There was a woollen mill at Pont Dolgarrog and a local sawmill produced railway sleepers for the new railways being built during the 19thC. In 1907 an aluminium works was built here utilising water from upland reservoirs to provide cheap hydro-electricity to run the mill. During World War II aircraft parts were made here. The works provided regular employment for the area and the village grew accordingly. Sadly it closed in 2007 and the site has now been prepared for future redevelopment. All that remains is the hydro-electric power station, one of the largest in Wales, which now provides power for about 15,000 homes each year. Originally water to power the station was supplied by a single pipeline from Llyn Eigau. Now it is delivered by two separate pipelines from Coedty and Cowlyd reservoirs.

As well as the aluminium works the village is associated with the worst dam disaster in Welsh history. On 2nd November 1925 after heavy rain the dam of Llyn Eigau high up in the mountains was breached, and water cascaded down the hillside destroying part of Dolgarrog and depositing huge boulders. Fortunately only 16 people died as most villagers were at the village hall watching a mobile cinema. This disaster led to changes in the design and building of dams.

19 Dolgarrog to Pontwgan

3¼ miles

After a short informative waymarked trail commemorating the dam disaster the route follows minor roads and paths to cross the Afon Dulyn in a small wooded valley. It then continues to the hamlet of Llanbedr-y-cennin, before heading north east to join a riverside path to the hamlet of Pontwgan, less than a mile from Rowen and a stop on the no.19 bus route.

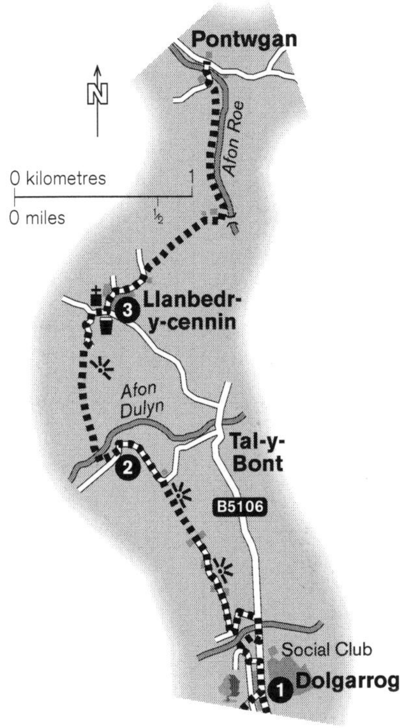

1 Walk north along the pavement alongside the B5106 then turn left up a road opposite Dolgarrog & District Social Club. Take a signposted path up a rough lane on the right. On the bend follow the signposted path ahead through trees, then go down its right fork past the Old Falls bed on the right, soon rising to a seat and information board above the river. Follow the path down through the trees to another information board by the road. Turn left along the pavement, over the river then turn left up a narrow no through road, soon enclosed by woodland. Shortly the road bends sharp right past Ceunant, a pottery, by a side road, then continues through woodland and past other houses. It then becomes a rougher undulating access lane – *soon with a good view across the valley* – passes Bron Haul and ends at the garage and outbuildings of nearby Ty Newydd. Follow the waymarked path through the garden edge beneath the house to a kissing gate. Go across the part bracken covered field to a hidden ladder-stile in the left-hand corner. Go along the field edge to another ladder-stile and across the next large field – *with a good view to Tal-y-Bont and the river Conwy* – to a gate in the corner onto a road by a farm. (The road leads right to nearby Tal-y-Bont.) Turn left up the narrow road passing beneath houses. Shortly it bends left, then almost immediately right at a facing gate.

2 After a few yards, just beyond a yellow grit container on the right you will find a path entering the trees parallel with the road. Follow the path along the top of the wooded valley, down to a large footbridge over the river and up past a ladder-stile to a gate. Continue along the tree-lined path, past a ladder-stile and an open view above a farm.

The narrow, now hedge-lined, path – *offering good views along the Conwy valley* – shortly becomes a green then concrete track which descends to an access lane by cottages. Follow it left to a junction. Turn right down the road into Llanbedr-y-cennin to reach the junction by Ye Olde Bull Inn. *The village, which lies on a drovers' route across the Carneddau mountains, is also known for Ffynnon Bedr, a holy well said to have curative properties.*

3 Turn left up the road past St Peter's medieval church, terraced cottages then a side road. Continue down the road. On the bend by Cennin Cottage go through the gate ahead to follow the signposted path along a track past Primrose Bank Cottage to cross a ladder-stile. Follow the tree boundary on your left down to cross another ladder-stile, then go down the next field edge to cross a ladder-stile on the right just before a house. Descend through trees to a gate and on past the end of large outbuildings. Turn left along the side of the lower outbuilding to a gate then keep ahead to cross a ladder-stile by the river. Cross the farm's access lane and the stile opposite, and follow the stiled riverside path through three fields, before angling away from the river to follow the fence round a small wood and up to a ladder-stile in the top field corner onto a road. Follow it right over the river to a junction in the small hamlet of Pontwgan, less than 1 mile from Rowen.

PONTWGAN TO CONWY

11, 9½, 8¼ or 6¾ miles

The trail continues through the varied attractive countryside of the lower Conwy Valley to Conwy. It offers choices of routes both to the attractive woodland of Parc Maw and onwards to the medieval walled town, enabling you to tailor your itinerary according to interest and requirements.

20 Pontwgan to Parc Mawr

From Pontwgan the trail continues to Parc Mawr, owned by the Woodland Trust, by two interesting routes. **Route A** (4¾ miles) takes a longer meandering approach, first visiting a 13thC church on the site of the Roman fort of Canovium. Afterwards it heads to the river Conwy where the bridge crosses to Tal-y-cafn at an ancient strategic crossing point of the river. It then follows field and woodland paths, and quiet country lanes across attractive undulating countryside. **Route B** (2 miles) takes a shorter more direct approach via the attractive village of Rowen, with its country inn and tea-rooms.

Route A

4¾ miles

1 Turn right and follow the road past a side road to the B5106 opposite the entrance to Caer Rhun Hall. Turn right. Go along the grass verge past Caer Rhun farm, then just beyond the cemetery sign take a minor road signposted to the 13thC St Mary's church. Go along the narrow road – *with a good view south down the wooded Conwy valley, and increasingly of the river.* Shortly the road passes between two oak trees marking the south west corner of the fort, with the ramparts visible on either side, and continues to St Mary's church.

The delightful ancient church dates from the 13thC and contains many later interesting features which are detailed in an available information sheet. Outside are yew trees said to be over a thousand years old. Canovium, built in the mid 70s AD, was an auxiliary fort linking Deva (Chester) and Segontium (Caernarfon). It was abandoned around 139-142 AD but some activity continued until the late 4thC.

2 After visiting the church cross a stile and continue along an access track offering a good view of the river. *Shortly down to your right at the edge of the estuary are the remains of an old dock.* After a gate leave the track to cross a stile ahead at the corner of a wood. Go along the field edge, past the bottom of a strip of woodland, then continue across a sloping field to a stile to enter Coed yr Arw. Follow the path through the mature woodland to a ladder-stile into a field. Go along the field edge to a gate in the corner to reach Tal-y-cafn-uchaf farm – *with a view ahead of the bridge over the* *river.* Go through the waymarked gate ahead, then angle left to pass round the large barn and on between the house and outbuildings. Descend its stony access track beneath Gronant cottage and follow it close by the river to reach a road. Turn right past modern houses built on the site of the former Ferryboat Inn to reach a side road at the bridge over the river.

This has been an important crossing point of the river since Roman times when it was part of the Roman road connecting garrisons at Deva (Chester), nearby Canovium and Segontium (Caernarfon). Nearby is a small man-made mound known as Bryn Castell, said to have been a tower outpost of Canovium or a 6thC Welsh fortress to guard the river. From the early 14thC a ferry operated across the river here, servicing the road from Conwy to Chester, and the drovers' route from Anglesey. Cattle would cross here at low tide, or later be carried across on a large floating platform. Eventually in 1897 the ferry was replaced by a steel toll bridge. The present bridge, which stands on the original piers, dates from 1977/78. On its far side is Tal y Cafn, where there was once an important freight depot on the Conwy Valley railway line, alongside the station. There is a former coaching inn of the same name, which offers meals and accommodation. Opposite is the former Roman road and later main medieval road which went via Eglwysbach to Chester.

3 First go a little way over the bridge for views along the river, then go along the side road. Shortly at a stone cottage the road rises steadily alongside a wood. Soon go through a waymarked gate on the left and up the edge of the large field – *with good views south to the foothills and the Carneddau mountains beyond* – to a gate. Go up the next field edge, then at the fence corner keep ahead to pass beneath the small part gorse covered small rocky top of Bryn-cwn and on to a stile to reach a minor road by a house. Follow it left, then on the bend go through an iron gate ahead. Go up the enclosed path, through two further gates, then up the field edge, later angling right up through trees to a ladder-stile. Bear right a few yards, then pass through gorse and to the right of an ivy covered stone ruin – *with a good view west to Tal-y-fan and the Carneddau range.* Keep ahead then follow the boundary on your right down the field to a ladder-stile onto the B5106.

4 Cross the road and follow the verge left, then turn right between Preswylfa and Haulfryn along a single track road. Follow this attractive narrow country road past other cottages. Later, just before the road descends through woodland, take a signposted path on the left along Glyn Bach's access track. Just past the house turn right on a waymarked path up to a gate between outbuildings. Keep ahead through the attractive garden to a kissing gate, then down to another into Glyn Parc. Follow the path down through mixed mature woodland to a road junction. Go along the road opposite signposted to Henryd, then

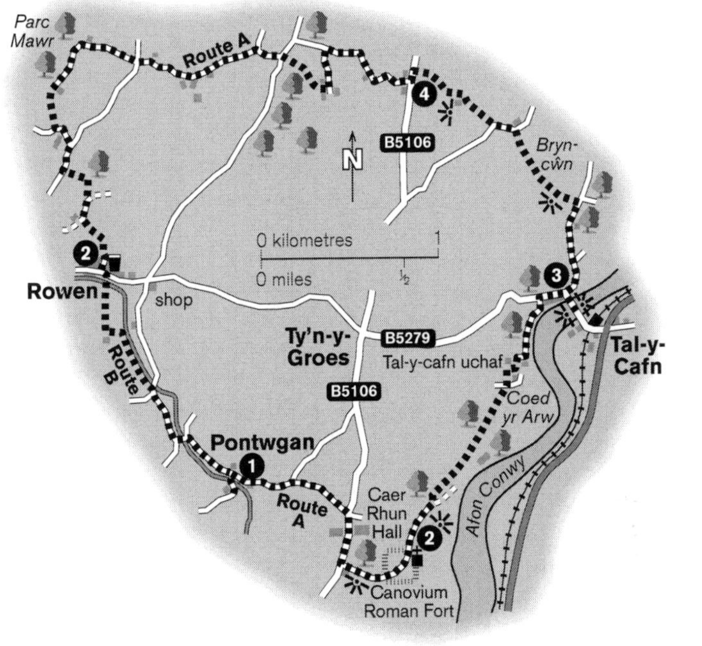

turn left along a side road. Follow it past Gwern Borter Manor and on towards the wooded slope of Parc Mawr. At a junction turn right. Go past the driveway to Tyddyn-mawr and up the narrow hedged lane ahead past Rowen scout camp to where it becomes the access track to Nant y Coed. Here is the gated entrance to Parc Mawr woodland.

Route B

2 miles

1 Turn left along the road, soon crossing the river. Just before another bridge over the river, take a signposted path through a kissing gate on the left. Walk along the edge of the long and narrowing field by the river to cross a ladder-stile. Bear left across the field to go through a gateway by an old farm. Turn right along a walled gated green track to Pen y Bont, then cross a footbridge over the Afon Roer to reach the centre of Rowen. Turn left. *With its neat stone cottages Rowen is one of the prettiest villages in the Conwy Valley. It once had several mills and inns, but only the Ty Gwyn, popular with walkers, remains. From here the former Roman road from Canovium, then drovers' route rises west across an upland landscape rich in evidence of early settlers: standing stones, burial chambers and an hillfort.*

2 Just beyond the Ty Gwyn Hotel and tearooms, then right along an adjoining lane. At its end angle left

St Mary's church, Caerhun

across a large stony area to cross an old iron ladder-stile by a gate. Keep ahead along the field, soon joining a stony track to pass through a gateway in an old wall. Continue along the track, soon bending left to a ladder-stile/gate. Just beyond bear right and follow the old field boundary down to cross a ladder-stile ahead. Turn right along a stony track and on the bend cross a ladder-stile ahead. Go along the field edge to cross another ladder-stile in the corner, then follow the raised path up alongside a fence to a narrow road. Follow it right, then take a signposted path up an access lane on the left. Just past Llwyn-onn cross a large ladder-stile on the right. Angle left up the field to the top left hand corner to go through a gate just beyond. *Pause to enjoy a good view along the Conwy valley.* Follow the boundary on your right to the field corner to cross a fence and small stone footbridge over a stream at the corner of Parc Mawr wood. Go along the green track ahead to pass nearby Nant y Coed and follow its access track beneath the wood to where it becomes a lane. Here is the gated entrance to Parc Mawr woodland.

21 Parc Mawr to Conwy

6¼ or 4¾ miles

From Parc Mawr there is a choice of routes to Conwy.

Route A (6¼ miles) takes a longer, more demanding, but rewarding upland approach. It first follows an ancient highway, which connected the Conwy valley with routes across the hills, up through the attractive woodland then open hillside to remote St Celynin's church, one of the oldest in Snowdonia. It then enters attractive open upland country once occupied by early man and now grazed by wild ponies, reaching a height of 1148 feet/350 metres. The trail follows a delightful track north across the upland pasture, enjoying extensive views, later descending to pass a small shallow lake and continuing to the top of historic Sychnant Pass. After a short section of the waymarked North Wales Path, it continues along the superb rocky ridge of Conwy Mountain (800 feet/244 metres), passing through an Iron Age hillfort, then makes a spectacular descent towards Conwy, with stunning views. (Following the North Wales Path across the southern slopes of Conwy Mountain is a lower alternative option.)

Route B (4¾ miles) takes a more direct approach. It first passes through the edge of Parc Mawr, then heads to the village of Henryd. Later, after rising through the edge of Conwy Touring Park, it continues across farmland offering great views of the river Conwy to reach a prominent viewpoint of Conwy and its castle at the finish.

Route A

6¼ miles

1 Go through the gate into Parc Mawr to an information board. Follow the wide stony path up through the wood to eventually leave it by a gate and continue ahead up an enclosed stony path. Shortly it becomes a delightful narrow walled green track, which rises steadily – *offering views back to the Conwy valley* – to reach St Celynin's church.

The church, dating from the 12thC, is an attractive and simple building of great character, standing at 951 feet/290 metres at a junction of several old paths, including the main route from the Conwy valley across the foothills to Penmaenmawr and westwards to Anglesey and Caernarfon. For centuries it has served this scattered upland community, and despite its remoteness, summer services are still held here. In the south corner of the churchyard is a rectangular holy well, which was renowned for its power to heal sick children. Near the churchyard gate an inn once stood which served the many travellers and drovers that used to pass by.

After visiting the church continue along the green track, past a ladder-stile. When the track bends right go through a gate ahead and follow a narrow green track up past a nearby house – *soon with a view of Tal-y-fan ahead* – to a gate into Open Access land by sheepfolds. Go through another gate ahead and follow the

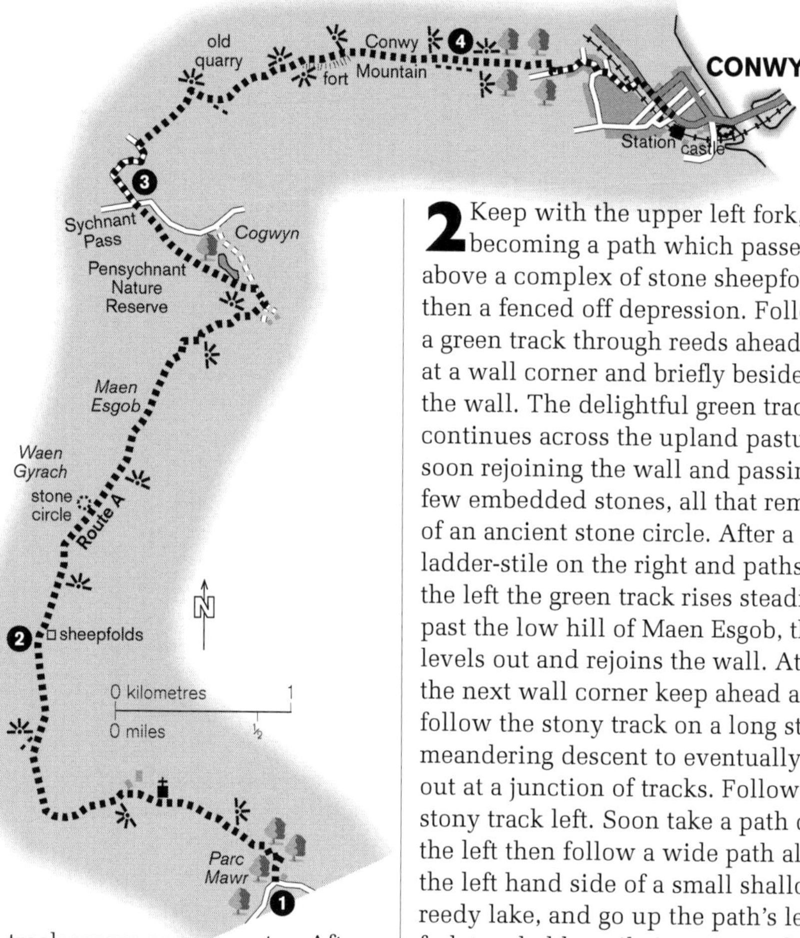

green track across open country. After about 150 yards as the track bends and rises half-left take a path on the right angling away from the track through an area of heather and gorse to cross a stream between two wall corners ahead. Follow a path close by the wall on your right across open upland pasture, later joining a green track which continues north – *offering good views ahead to The Great Orme and across the Conwy estuary to Deganwy, with Conwy castle prominent.* Shortly the track begins to descend and splits.

2 Keep with the upper left fork, soon becoming a path which passes above a complex of stone sheepfolds, then a fenced off depression. Follow a green track through reeds ahead at a wall corner and briefly beside the wall. The delightful green track continues across the upland pasture, soon rejoining the wall and passing a few embedded stones, all that remains of an ancient stone circle. After a ladder-stile on the right and paths on the left the green track rises steadily past the low hill of Maen Esgob, then levels out and rejoins the wall. At the next wall corner keep ahead and follow the stony track on a long steady meandering descent to eventually level out at a junction of tracks. Follow the stony track left. Soon take a path on the left then follow a wide path along the left hand side of a small shallow reedy lake, and go up the path's left fork to a ladder-stile into Pensychnant Nature Reserve. Follow the path down to a small covered reservoir and along the edge of a wood, past the waymarked North Wales Path, to a gate to reach the road at the top of Sychnant Pass. *This is the most northerly pass in Snowdonia National Park. The road through it was built in the 18thC as part of the mail coach route. Inns opened at Capelulo, which became an important coaching stop for travellers until a new coastal road was opened in the 1820s. Despite* *loss of the passing trade, it became a popular place for Victorian visitors who enjoyed horse-drawn trips.*

3 Take the signposted North Wales Path along a rough lane opposite, passing beneath crags and rising, then becoming a stony track. Follow it to a finger post then turn right with the North Wales Path to a nearby gate. Go up the stony track ahead, shortly descending to a crossroad of green tracks by a waymark post. Keep ahead to reach another waymark post – *with a view ahead of the quarried hillside and the Great Orme beyond.* Here turn right up the North Wales Path, then at another post where the North Wales Path bears right, keep ahead up the stony path. At a crossroad of paths angle left up the stony path to another path junction. Turn left along the wide path, climbing steadily, soon with a choice of paths onto Conwy Mountain ridge – *offering extensive coastal views.* Go along the higher ridge to pass through Caer Seion hillfort with its stone entrance visible below. *It was used between 2300-1900 years ago and contained about 50 round buildings.* Shortly the ridge path makes a rocky descent – *with a good view down to Conwy castle.* An easier option is to follow an adjoining path on the left. The path then levels out – *with a view down to Conwy and Deganwy marinas.* Shortly it descends again and bends down to the end of a large rock slab.

4 Just before a North Wales Path waymark post take a wide path leading left, soon descending steadily along the ridge then by a woodland boundary. At the wall corner the path bends down and round to a ladder-stile above a house, then descends to an access lane at the outskirts of Conwy. Follow it left down past houses, then at the junction turn right down and up Mountain Road. At a junction turn left along Cadnant Park, soon crossing the deep railway cutting. At the junction turn right then pass through the western gate of the medieval walled town. Continue down the road to a small square with a columned water fountain at the entrance to the cobbled High Street.

Route B

4¾ miles

1 Go through the gate into Parc Mawr to an information board and up the path a few yards, then turn right to follow an undulating path along the edge of the attractive woodland. Later when the now wide path/track begins to climb, take a narrower path angling off on the right past a post indicating no horse riders. After crossing a stream, it rises gently through the trees, then passes through a wall gap. Descend the stepped path and continue along the wood edge passing behind Tanrallt Farm to descend to a small gate onto its access track. Follow it left to a road. Turn left past a car parking area and continue up the road, then cross a waymarked stile on the right. Follow the path down through gorse, soon bending left down through woodland to a stile. Go past a house and outbuilding and down its access track. When it meets a concrete driveway go through a gateway directly opposite. Go down the field to a ladder-stile, then follow the left-hand edge of the next field to a gap in the field corner to cross an old iron ladder-stile beyond. Follow the right hand field edge to another iron ladder-stile and on to a small gate to reach a road junction. Go along the road ahead into nearby Henryd. At the junction turn left through the village, then continue along the attractive country road. After nearly ½ mile you pass a road on the left to reach a white house on the bend.

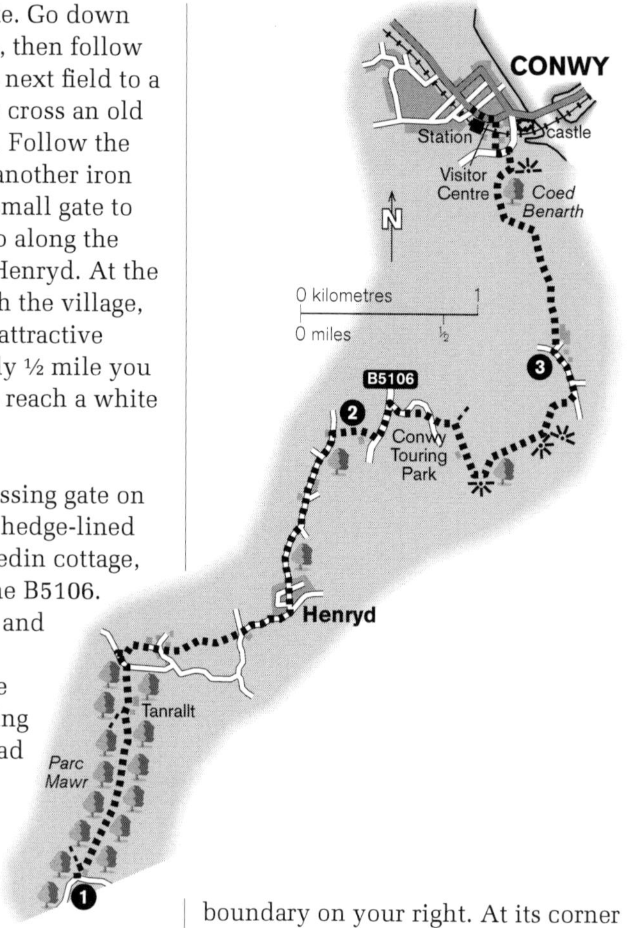

2 Here go through a kissing gate on the right and up the hedge-lined path, past Ysgubor Cyffredin cottage, then up a field edge to the B5106. Cross the road with care and walk left along the grass verge for 150 yards to the entrance to Conwy Touring Park. Go up its access road to a kissing gate on its bend, then follow the path up to rejoin the access road. Follow the signposted wide tree-lined path ahead to cross a large metal ladder-stile on the right by a finger post into the caravan park. After a few yards bear left to pass through a large gap in a high hedge. Keep ahead through the caravan park to follow a rough access road passing to the left of a toilet block. At the end of the park keep ahead along a stony track passing through a tree boundary and bending left to reach a great viewpoint overlooking the Conwy valley and the river. Here go through a kissing gate on the left. Angle across to join the boundary on your right. At its corner turn right. After about 20 yards, just below a group of stones, go half-left across the mid-slopes to a fence (stile requested). Continue in the same direction across the mid-slopes of the next field down to a gate in the fence ahead (stile requested). Go across the next field to another ladder-stile – *enjoying panoramic views* – then head towards a small quarry ahead. Just before it bear right along a farm track to a minor road. Continue up the road past the entrance to Cymnyd Uchaf, then Pine Lodge.

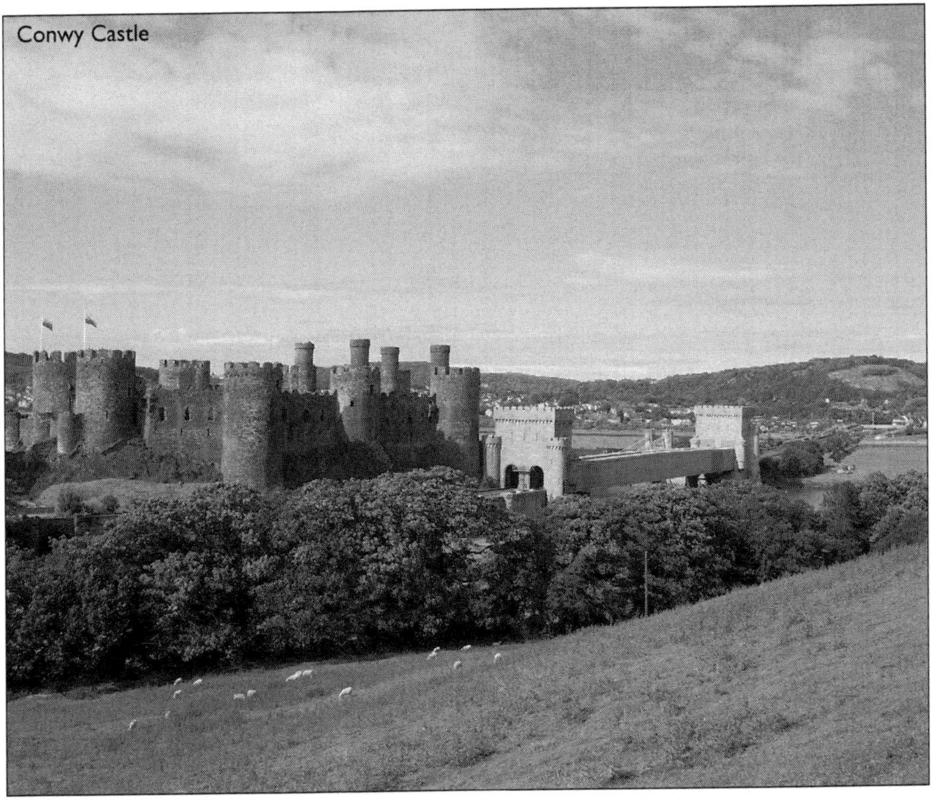
Conwy Castle

3 Cross a ladder-stile on the right by a farm entrance and go through an adjoining gate. Go along the field past the farm to a ladder-stile, then across the next field to another ladder-stile. Go across the third field, past an old ladder-stile and on past a water trough in the fence ahead to a small gate and ladder-sile at the end of an area of gorse. Angle right across the next field to another ladder-stile – *enjoying good views across to Conwy Mountain.* Turn left along the field edge down to a kissing gate by a water trough in the corner. Cross a stile ahead and follow the path down the edge of Coed Benarth to a ladder-stile at the wood edge. *Ahead is a stunning view of nearby Conwy Castle, Stephenson's tubular railway bridge, the town walls, and over the estuary to Deganwy Marina, and further still, the Great Orme.* Descend the field to a kissing gate onto the road. Cross to the pavement opposite and follow it left, then turn across the river into the car park. Keep straight ahead to go through an underpass below the railway line. Turn left up steps to pass through an archway between towers to reach a fingerpost. Go along the pavement past the nearby Conwy Visitor Centre, then bus shelters to reach the entrance to the cobbled High Street on the right by a small square featuring a columned water fountain.

CONWY TO CONWY BAY AND RETURN

5 or 4¼ miles

The trail takes you through the historic heart of Conwy past old houses and its imposing castle, then heads to its Marina before continuing along the edge of Conwy Morfa, a protected area of sand dunes, to the mouth of the estuary and Conwy Bay. It then returns across the golf course to Marina Village to rejoin the outward route, before passing through Bodlonded Woods, a local nature reserve. The trail finishes at Conwy quayside after an exhilarating walk along the medieval town walls, or directly if preferred.

The stunning medieval fortified walled town of Conwy standing near the mouth of the Afon Conwy estuary against a backdrop of mountains, is a designated World Heritage Site. Its impressive late 13thC castle was built for Edward I to strengthen his conquest of Wales, and the walls, over ¾ mile in length, originally with 22 towers enclosed a new town occupied by English settlers. Crossing the estuary are two historic bridges built by renowned engineers: Thomas Telford's graceful suspension bridge (1822-26) and the adjacent tubular railway bridge built by Robert Stephenson which opened in 1849. Conwy was once a busy port with a long association with pearl fishing from freshwater mussels found in the estuary. In the early 19thC large numbers of Conwy pearls were sent to London jewellers. Pearl mussels are rare nowadays, but a few licenced boats still operate in the estuary, gathering mussels for the table. Today the estuary and marina are home to many small pleasure boats and yachts, and the town remains a mecca for visitors.

22 The final section

5 or 4¼ miles

1 From the water fountain go along High Street past Plas Mawr, an Elizabethan town house, dating from 1576, down to its end. *On the right hand corner is Aberconwy House, a 14thC merchant's house, believed to be the oldest house in Conwy.* Cross to the Civic Hall opposite then turn right along Castle Street past shops. At its end with the impressive castle ahead continue along the pavement to go through an archway ahead and on to cross the road leading down to the quayside. First continue over Pont Conwy to enjoy views along the estuary. *Nearby are Telford's suspension bridge and Stephenson's tubular railway bridge.* Retrace your steps then follow the pathway down to the quayside. Go past Conwy Mussels, toilets, the Liverpool Arms and the Smallest House to pass under the town walls. Go up the road then turn right on the signposted North Wales Path between Glan-y-Afon and Shore Cottage to the start of Marine Walk.

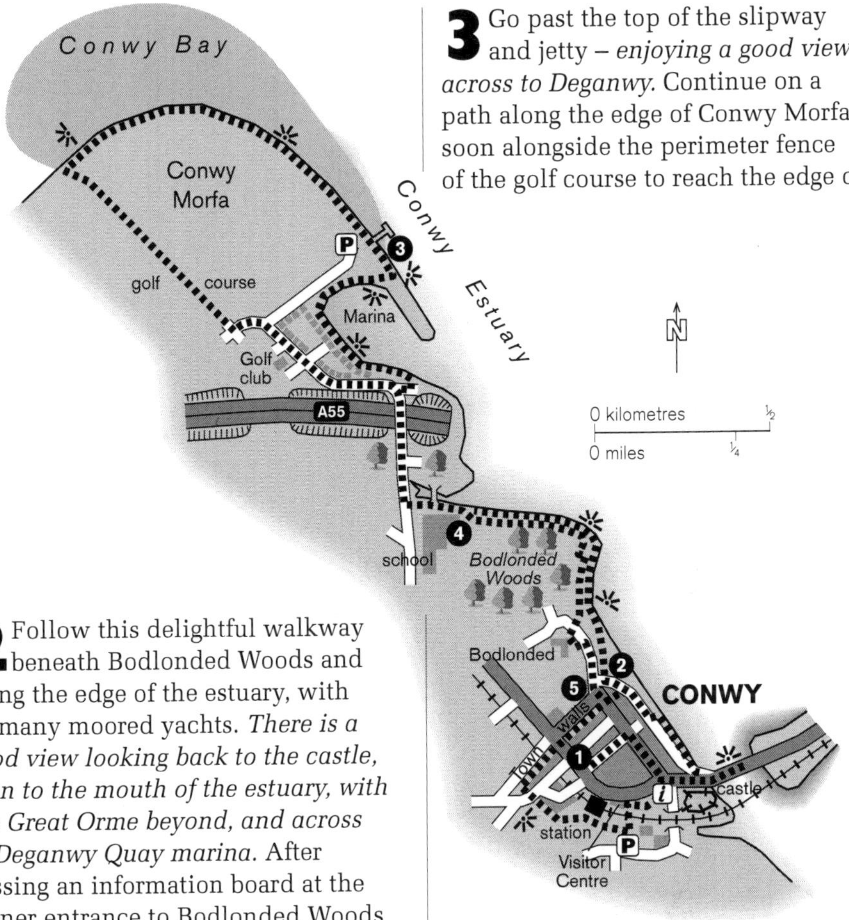

2 Follow this delightful walkway beneath Bodlonded Woods and along the edge of the estuary, with its many moored yachts. *There is a good view looking back to the castle, then to the mouth of the estuary, with the Great Orme beyond, and across to Deganwy Quay marina.* After passing an information board at the corner entrance to Bodlonded Woods continue along the walkway past the blue pedestrian bridge to reach the entrance to Ysgol Aberconwy. Follow the road right, soon passing over the A55. At Marina Village turn right to reach The Mulberry (a good refreshment stop) and access to the marina. *It was created from a specially excavated casting basin, where tube sections of the Conwy tunnel (1991) were built before being floated into position in the river.* Continue round the edge of the marina to its far corner by the estuary, then turn left.

3 Go past the top of the slipway and jetty – *enjoying a good view across to Deganwy.* Continue on a path along the edge of Conwy Morfa, soon alongside the perimeter fence of the golf course to reach the edge of Conwy Bay, an extensive area of sand at low tide. *Here you have a good view of the Great Orme and Anglesey.* The path now bends away from the estuary above the rocky shoreline – *with views to Conwy Mountain and the quarried coastal hills above Penmaenmawr. Conwy Morfa has an interesting history. During the 19thC people worked here extracting pearls from mussels. In 1898 the Royal Welsh Fusiliers had a camp here and evidence of their rifle range remains. In 1944 about 900 men worked on* *the Morfa in great secrecy building sections of the floating harbour, codenamed Mulberry, which was used in D-Day landings in Normandy.* At an old concrete rifle butt turn left to join a nearby stony track. Follow it across the middle of the golf course, then an access road left to the nearby road at Marina Village. Follow it past the entrance to the golf club, then at a roundabout continue along the road ahead to join your outward route. Follow it back to the information board at the corner of Bodlonded Woods.

4 Enter the Bodlonded Woods – *created by Albert Wood, one of Conwy's great benefactors, who lived at nearby Bodlondeb mansion, built for his family in 1877 and now Council Offices.* Angle left to follow a path up the wood edge above Marine Walk, soon passing a seat at good viewpoint looking towards the mouth of the estuary. Continue with the path along the wood edge, past another seat then a path rising right. At another path junction by a small waymark post turn left down through the trees, then right along the wide path. After passing below a greenhouse (Butterfly Jungle) descend steps on the left and follow a pathway across gardens offering good views then up to a nearby road. Angle right to join a path opposite, with Bodlondeb Hall nearby, then follow formal paths round the left roadside edge of parkland to rejoin the road by seats. Follow it right to a gateway by a lodge.

5 Here you have a choice. The easier option is to turn left down Lower Gate Street to join your outward route back to the quayside, perhaps for a celebratory drink at the Liverpool Arms, fish and chips, or a boat trip on the river. A more interesting finale is to extend the walk along the town walls before making your way to the quayside. For this option go to the main road ahead and follow the pavement left through the nearby archway, then go up steps onto the town walls. First descend to the end overlooking the river, then return to follow the western walls up to a corner tower, from where there is a dramatic descent – *with a good view to the castle and south along the Conwy valley.* Later the walls level out and you are forced to descend steps. At the bottom – *with the entrance to the station just ahead* – turn left to pass under the wall and follow the access lane (Twr Llewelyn) down to a car park. Immediately turn left to go through the underpass below the railway, then go up steps to pass through an archway between towers, with the Visitor Centre nearby. Climb up the right tower and walk along the final section of wall. After descending go along the car park edge to the castle entrance and Tourist Information Centre. Descend to the lower entrance and cross to the pavement opposite beneath the castle. Use the nearby Pelican crossing and continue to the quayside for that celebratory drink.

Linear walks

The generally good local public transport network allows the Conwy Valley Way to be undertaken as linear day/half-day walks of variable length, which enables people of all ages and abilities to enjoy the long distance trail at convenience. Frequent buses on some sections enable local walkers or one-centre visitors to undertake linear walks without a car.

Bus services can change at any time, so please check current available services and times before planning any walk. Detailed bus timetables are available from relevant local authorities and from Tourist Information Centres (See the Transport section in Guidance Notes and Useful Information).

I have broken the trail down into 16 linear walks, but most can be combined to make longer day walks if required. Use the buses indicated then follow the appropriate section of the Conwy Valley Way back to the starting point.

Walk 1 Llandudno to Deganwy (7 miles)
Follow instructions in section 1 to Deganwy then take a choice of regular buses back to Llandudno.

Walk 2 Deganwy via Conwy RSPB Nature Reserve to Llandudno Junction (4 miles) or to Glan Conwy (5½ miles)
Follow instructions in section 2 to Glan Conwy and catch either the X1 or no. 25 bus back. Alternatively for a shorter walk finish at Llandudno Junction, from where there is a choice of buses or train to Deganwy.

Walk 3 Glan Conwy to Eglwysbach (5¾ miles)
This walk follows the trail to just beyond Graig, then extends south to Eglwysbach.
From a bus stop by the church in Eglwysbach (car parking in Maes Llan opposite) take the no. 25 bus to Glan Conwy then follow instructions in section 3 to Graig. At crossroads turn right past the bus shelter and follow Ffordd Ty Gwyn down into the valley to cross over the river (see map on page 20). Continue up the road. On the bend just before a farm turn left on a signposted path along a narrow no through road, passing beneath mature woodland. After passing Bryn Hir continue along a hedge-lined track, soon descending and bending to cross a footbridge over the river. Follow the path above the stream, soon crossing it to reach the village.

Walk 4 Tal-y-Cafn to Llanrwst (9½ or 8 miles)
This walk accesses the trail following an ancient route from Tal-y-Cafn. (See section 20 – Route A – for information on Tal-y-Cafn)
Take the X1 bus from Watling Street in Llanrwst to Tal-y-Cafn. From the former roadside coaching inn of the same name take the minor road (Ffordd Penrhyd) opposite, up to a junction. *This road which leads to Eglwysbach was part of the former Roman road from nearby Canovium garrison to Deva (Chester) and later the main route from Conwy to Chester.* Bear left up past houses. At the next junction turn right up Ffordd Llyn Syberi. Now follow the instructions for the Conwy Valley Way from the 6th sentence in paragraph 1 of section 4 back to Llanrwst. The walk can be split into two shorter walks by utilising the bus stop at Maenan Abbey on the A470.

Walk 5 Glan Conwy to Llanrwst (14½ or 13 miles)
Take the X1 bus from Watling Street in Llanrwst to Glan Conwy and follow instructions in sections 3,4 & 5 back to Llanrwst.

Walk 6 Llanrwst to Betws-y-Coed (9 miles)
From the bus stand just beyond the railway station in Betws-y-Coed take the X1 bus to Watling Street, Llanrwst. Follow the one-way road round to the main road by Pont Fawr. Now follow instructions in sections 6 & 7 to Betws-y-Coed.

Walk 7 Betws-y-Coed to Conwy Falls (3½ or 3¼ miles)
A short but interesting walk with a choice of routes, before leaving the trail to descend to the Conwy Falls Cafe, from where paths run to the waterfalls (a small entry charge payable). Another option from here is to follow the B4406 to minor crossroads, turn right to join section 14 of the trail at the former woollen mill and Roman Bridge. Later follow either route A or B in section 15 back to Betws-y-Coed. This creates a good circular walk of either 10 or 7½ miles.
From Betws-y-Coed follow instructions in paragraphs 1 & 2 of section 8, chosing either Route A or B. When both routes reach a minor road, follow it down to the A5. Cross the road with care to reach the nearby junction with the B4406 by the Conwy Falls Café, from where you can catch the no. 64 bus from Penmachno back to Betws-y-Coed.

Walk 8 Betws-y-Coed to Penmachno via Ysbyty Ifan (10¾ or 11 miles)
Take the 64 bus from Penmachno to Betws-y-Coed. Now follow instructions in section 8 & 9 to Ysbyty Ifan then section 13 from Ysbyty Ifan to Penmachno (Route B).

Walk 9 Ysbyty Ifan to Penmachno via Llyn Conwy (12¾ miles)
From Betws-y-Coed take the 8.50 am no. 70 bus (Tuesday, Wednesdays & Fridays only except public holiday) to Ysbyty Ifan. Now follow instructions in sections 10, 11 & 12 to Penmachno (Route A). Catch the no. 64 bus from Penmachno to Betws-y-Coed.
Alternatively park in Penmachno and take the no. 64 bus (8.10 am) to Betws-y-Coed, then the no. 70 bus (8.50 am) to Ysbyty Ifan.

Walk 10 Penmachno to Betws-y-Coed (8 or 5½ miles)
From the bus stand just beyond the railway station in Betws-y-Coed take the no. 64 bus to Penmachno. Now follow instructions in sections 14 & 15 selecting either Route A via Llyn Elsi, or Route B via Fairy Glen.

Walk 11 Betws-y-Coed to Llanrwst (5¾ miles)
From Watling Street in Llanrwst take the X1 bus (Blaenau Ffestiniog) to Betws-y-Coed railway station. Go along the station platform, cross the footbridge over the railway line and follow the pathway round the buffet car cafe to the road beyond. Follow it right to nearby St Michael's church. Now follow instructions from the third sentence in paragraph 1 of section 16 to Llyn Parc, then follow paragraph 1 of Route B in section 17 to Llanrwst.

Walk 12 Betws-y-Coed to Trefriw (12¾, 11¼ or 8¼ miles)
From a bus stop opposite Trefriw Woollen Mill (car park nearby) take the no. 19 bus to Betws-y-Coed railway station (Sundays/Public Holidays) or take the 19 bus to Watling Street in Llanrwst, then take the X1 bus (Blaenau Ffestiniog) to Betws-y-Coed. Make your way to St Michael's church as described in Walk 11, then follow instructions from the third sentence in paragraph 1 of section 16 to Llyn Parc. From here, in section 17, follow either the longer meandering Route A via upland lakes or the shorter Route B via Llanrwst .

Walk 13 Trefriw to Dolgarrog (5¾ or 4¾ miles)
From Dolgarrog take the no. 19 bus to Trefriw Woollen Mill, then follow instructions in section 18, later choosing either Route A or B to Dolgarrog.

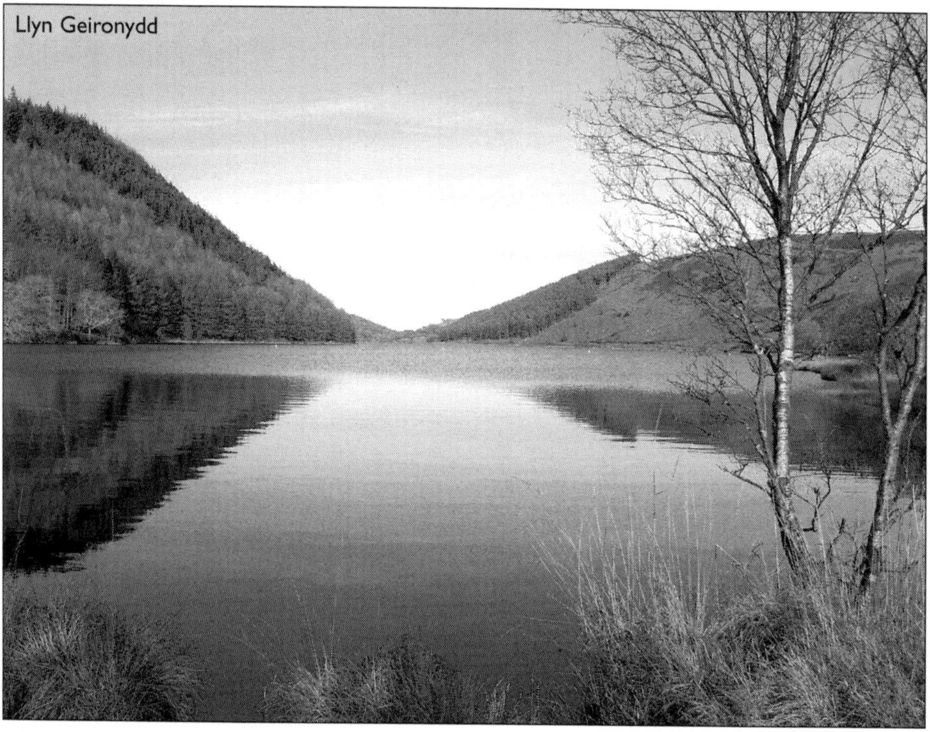

Walk 14 Dolgarrog to Rowen (4¼ miles)
Just after entering the main village of Rowen there is roadside parking on the right by the first houses. Walk back along the road to a bus stop near the crossroads by the PO/shop. Take the 19 bus to the centre of Dolgarrog near the PO/stores. Now follow instructions in section 19 to Pontwgan, then paragraph 1 of Route B in section 20 to Rowen.

Walk 15 Rowen to Conwy via either St Celynin's church and Sychnant Pass or Henryd (7¼ or 5¾ miles)
From the bus stand M by the railway station in Conwy take the 19 bus to Rowen. Now follow instructions in paragraph 2 of Route B in section 20 to Parc Mawr, then either Route A or Route B in section 21 to Conwy.

Walk 16 Caerhun via Canovium Roman fort to Conwy (10½ or 9 miles)
From the bus stand M by the railway station in Conwy take the 19 to a bus stop on the B5106 by Caer Rhun Hall. Now follow instructions in the 2nd sentence of paragraph 1 of Route A in section 20 to Parc Mawr, then either Route A or Route B in section 21 to Conwy.

Guidance Notes & Useful Information

General advice

In this guidebook I have divided the Conwy Valley Way into 22 short sections within 10 chapters. Each section contains the detailed route descriptions, accompanying maps and notes on local history etc. On some sections of the walk I have included a choice of routes that offer different features or benefits, so you can tailor the trail according to your interests and needs.

It is also possible to undertake the trail as two separate walks:

– a walk from Llandudno down the east side of the main valley to Betws-y-Coed, returning up the west side to Conwy – up to 73¾ miles in length.

– an extended circular walk from Betws-y-Coed of between 19¼ miles and 28¼ miles exploring the upper valley, Ysbyty Ifan and Penmachno.

For those wishing to undertake the trail as a continuous walk of 7 – 8 days, the daily stages will be determined as much by available accommodation on or near the trail as by level of fitness. It may be that you end a stage where you can catch a bus to available accommodation and return the following day by bus to continue the trail. It is recommended though that accommodation, especially where limited, is booked in advance.

The 12¾ mile section of the trail from Ysbyty Ifan to the source and on to Penmachno (Route A) is the only part of the walk that is a challenge to complete, namely

– the demanding nature of the wild remote tussocky/heather terrain on this section in the upper valley and around Llyn Conwy makes this only suitable for experienced and well equipped hill walkers who can cope with the demands of Open Access land.

– Ysbyty Ifan, despite its origins as a hospice for travellers in need, offers no facilities. This is not a problem for those continuing on the direct Route B to Penmachno or day walkers who can use two cars. The nearest known place to stay overnight is a b&b and campsite at Llwyn Onn Guesthouse at Rhydlydan 3¾ miles away (willing to pick up from Ysbyty Ifan).

However the village is currently served by an early morning bus no. 70

from Betws-y-Coed (8.50 am) on Tuesdays, Wednesdays and Fridays (Bank holidays excepted). An option therefore is that you plan your itinerary to make use of this limited service. Walk the trail from Betws-y-Coed to Penmachno following the delightful drovers route from Ysbyty Ifan to Penmachno (Route B). Take the no. 64 bus to Betws-y-Coed and stay overnight, then catch the no. 70 bus to Ysbyty Ifan to complete Route A. Alternatively overnight in Penmachno and take the early bus to Betws-y-Coed to catch the no. 70 bus to Ysbyty Ifan.

Given the nature of this valley walk and available public transport there is another way that the trail can be completed as a continuous walk, without carrying a full pack. From one or two accommodation bases, and by a combination of car and bus (or rail where appropriate) in both directions, or with careful planning, by bus alone, you can systematically complete each stage carrying only a day bag. I would particularly recommend this approach to those people wishing to camp – a method I have used successfully to complete several long distance walks. The linear walks linked to local bus services and designed for day walkers which are detailed in the previous chapter will help in your planning.

Although undertaking sections of the trail as day walks can be undertaken throughout the year, for those planning to walk the whole trail continuously, the best time is between Spring and late Autumn. Each season offers its own appeal. In Spring the trees and hedgerows are returning to life, the woods are full of bluebells and wild garlic, and birdlife is particularly active. Summer with its long hours of daylight and sunshine allows more time to linger and enjoy the scenery, but accommodation is at a premium during the school holidays. The changing colours of Autumn are especially delightful in this part-wooded valley.

Whenever you choose to walk the trail please remember to build sufficient time into your itinerary to visit and enjoy the many places of interest along the route. If you are planning to overnight at Betws-y-Coed after the short day's walking from Penmachno, you will have the opportunity to build in some additional local walking, say to visit the famous Miners Bridge. If staying at the youth hostel you can visit Swallow Falls opposite.

Good walking boots are required along with appropriate clothing to protect against the elements. Be prepared for any weather, which can vary from Spring snow to hot sunshine during the walk. The weather generally changes more rapidly in the hills than the coast, with rain and mist descending quickly. But do not forget the suntan cream – all-day walking in the sun unprotected can cause discomfort and be harmful. Carry plenty of drink and food, especially on those sections where facilities are limited or non-existent, and emergency equipment, including compass, map, whistle and small torch.

The route follows public Rights of Way or permissive paths and crosses designated land where walkers have the legal right of access under the CRoW Act 2000. Open Access land can be subject to restrictions and closure for land management or safety reasons for up to 28 days a year. Please respect any notices. Visit the Countryside Council for Wales web site (www.ccw.gov.uk) in advance to check on any temporary closures that may apply.

The route also passes through Gwydyr Forest Park, owned by the Forestry Commission, where walkers are welcome. Extending north from Penmachno via Betws-y-Coed to Trefriw the forest contains tracks, waymarked forest trails, old miners' paths and cycle trails. Please be aware that on occasions forest clearance work and other operations may require temporary closure of some areas, but any diversions will be signposted where possible.

Please remember that changes in details on the ground – i.e. new stiles and gates, field boundaries, path diversions etc can occur at any time. Also that the condition of paths can vary according to season and weather.

If you encounter any obstacles or other problems on rights of way please report these to Conwy County Borough Council Countryside Service and Rights of Way section (Tel 01492 574000 or via www.conwy.gov.uk).

Other matters relating to Gwydyr Forest Park can be referred to the Forest Office (01492 640578).

Maps

The route is covered by the following 1: 25000 scale Ordnance Survey maps:

Explorer Map OL17: Snowdon/Yr Wyddfa [Llandudno to just south of Betws-y-Coed]
Explorer Map OL18: Harlech, Porthmadog & Bala [Upper Conwy Valley]

The Countryside Code

Be safe - plan ahead and follow any signs
Leave gates and property as you find them
Protect plants and animals, and take your litter home
Keep dogs under close control
Consider other people
Please observe the Countryside Code and respect any ancient site visited.

Facilities

The Conwy Valley is a popular holiday area which is reflected in the overall good range of facilities available, but these will vary along the route. For the long distance walker the main considerations are overnight accommodation, evening meal options and refreshment stops/shops on or near the route. The internet is now a good source of information for planning your walk along with the area's Tourist Information Centres. The following information is a guide, but inevitably details will change. It is particularly sad that in the current economic climate village shops and pubs are under threat of closure. If planning to call at a pub en route I suggest you contact it in advance to check its opening times and whether it serves food.

Llandudno to Llandudno Junction

As a popular tourist destination this section offers a good range of accommodation and other facilities. On route there is a café on Great Orme's Head, one on West Shore, various refreshment options at Deganwy and Llandudno Junction, and a café at Conwy Nature Reserve.

Llandudno Junction to Llanrwst

Glan Conwy has two pubs (The Cross Keys and The Estuary) and a coffee shop in Snowdonia Nurseries. The section between Glan Conwy and Llanrwst is largely rural, but there is a café by the car park entrance at Bodnant Gardens. There is a pub (The Bee Inn) off the route at Eglwysbach, and later you pass Maenan Abbey Hotel on the A470, offering bar meals and accommodation. Llanrwst has a good range of facilities, including accommodation, shops, pubs etc.

Llanrwst to Betws-y-Coed

There are no refreshment facilities or shops between these two towns. Betws-y-Coed offers a good range of facilities including b&b's, pubs, cafés, restaurants, outdoor shops, campsites and a youth hostel 2 miles west of the village centre.

Betws-y-Coed to Ysbyty Ifan

There is the White Horse Inn at Capel Garmon. Conwy Falls café on the A5 and Rynys Farm campsite are just off the route. There is a lay-by café on the A5 near Pont Rhydlanfair, 100 yards off the route. Ysbyty Ifan has no shop, pub or known accommodation. However there is a b&b and campsite (with campers breakfasts) at Llwyn Onn Guesthouse (01690 770124) at Rhydlydan 3¾ miles away, with a local pub for evening meals. Llwyn Onn is willing to provide a pick up service from Ysbyty Ifan by prior arrangement. Please confirm at time of booking.

Ysbyty Ifan to Penmachno

Neither trail route has refreshment facilities between communities. It is particularly important that you carry food and drink on Route A which crosses wild upland country. Bus 64 can be caught at Carrog to Penmachno or Betws-y-Coed. In Penmachno The Eagles Inn (01690 760177) offers luxury bunkhouse accommodation, with bedding and tea/coffee making facilities provided, and a self-catering kitchen, but no evening meals. So you will have to carry food for your evening meal. Penmachno Hall and Ty Blaid offer b&b. Another option is to take the no. 64 bus to Betws-y-Coed, with its plentiful facilities, and return on it the following morning to resume your walk.

Betws-y-Coed to Trefriw

On Route A through Gwydwr Forest Parc to Trefriw there are toilets at Llyn Geirionydd and Crafnant car parks, and a seasonal café alongside Llyn Crafnant. Route B passes tea-rooms at Pont Fawr, Llanrwst and the town's other facilities are nearby. Trefriw has two pubs, a butchers/grocers (its steak pies are recommended), a newsagents, post office, cafés, including one in the woollen mill, b&b's, and hotels.

Trefriw to Conwy

There are no facilities on route between Trefriw and Dolgarrog except the Lord Newborough pub on the outskirts of Dolgarrog on Route B. There is a shop/PO in the village centre. Tal-y-Bont, just off the route, has a shop/ post office, pub, b&b and a backpackers barn (01492 660504). On the route there is Ye Olde Bull Inn in Llanbedr-y-cennin. In Rowen there is the Ty Gwyn Hotel and tearooms, a PO/shop, b&bs nearby and a youth hostel on the higher slopes above the village. At Tal-y-Cafn, a short walk across the bridge over the river, is an old coaching inn of the same name, offering meals and accommodation. There is a campsite at Conwy Touring Park on Route B. Conwy has a good range of facilities: b&b's, youth hostel, pubs, cafés, restaurants etc. On the last section to the mouth of the estuary there is The Mulberry pub at Conwy Marina.

Tourist Information Centres

The following offer information and an accommodation booking service:

Llandudno	01492 577577 – www.llandudno-tourism.co.uk
Conwy	01492 592248 – www.visitconwy.org.uk
Betws-y-coed	01690 710426 – www.betws-y-coed.co.uk

Transport

Both Llandudno and Conwy are easily accessible via the National Rail network from any part of the UK. and the National Express network.
The Conwy Valley Way is supported by easily accessible public transport throughout most of its length. The local bus services which I used to research the route were reliable, clean and comfortable. They offer good views of the countryside and communities they pass through, and are an enjoyable part of the visiting experience.
A comprehensive free Public Transport Information booklet is produced by Conwy County Borough Council twice a year. It details all local bus services and the Conwy Valley rail service and is available from local libraries, Tourist Information Centres, or direct from the Council (see contact details below).
As a guide these are the current services available but please remember that

Conwy Quay

they are subject to changes, so always check up to date timetables:

Bus services no's **13, 19, 25** and **X1** run regularly (*Mon-Sat*) between Llandudno Junction and Llandudno. The **13** and **19** offer a limited Sunday service. The no. **27** runs from Llandudno Junction to Conwy daily if overnighting there.

The **X1** runs regularly (*Mon-Sat*) between Betws-y-Coed and Llandudno via Llanrwst and Glan Conwy.

The no. **25** runs (*Mon-Sat*) between Eglwysbach and Llandudno via Glan Conwy with a limited Sunday service. The no. **84** operates a limited Sunday service between Glan Conwy, Llandudno Junction and Llandudno.
The Conwy Valley railway provides a limited number of trains between Llandudno and Betws-y-Coed (*Mon-Sat*) calling at Glan Conwy, Tal-y-Cafn, Dolgarrog/Maenan and Llanrwst.

The no. **64** runs (*Mon-Sat*) between Cwm Penmachno and Llanrwst via Betws-y-Coed. In the Machno valley it stops at Carrog, Penmachno, on the B4406 at minor crossroads (Penmachno woollen mill stop) near the former mill and the Roman Bridge, then at Conwy Falls Café.

The no. **69** has an early morning service from Llanrwst to Betws-y-Coed where it connects with the **70** to Ysbyty Ifan on Tuesday, Wednesday & Friday, except public holidays.

The western side of the Conwy valley is well served by the **19** bus service, which provides an hourly service (Mon-Sat) from Llandudno calling at Conwy, Dolgarrog, Trefriw and Llanrwst, and two-hourly to Rowan and Pontwgan. At Llanrwst you can take the hourly **X1** service to Betws-y-Coed. On Sundays the no. **19** provides a through service from Llandudno to Betws-y-Coed, with limited times for Rowen.

Public Transport Enquiries

Bws Conwy
Conwy County Borough Council
Conwy Business Centre
Llandudno Junction
LL31 9XX
01492 575469/575450 – www.conwy.gov.uk – email: bwsconwy@conwy.gov.uk

traveline: 0871 200 2233

National Rail: 08457 484950

National Express: 08705 8080

Other Kittiwake Guides by David Berry

Available at local bookshops and Tourist Information Centres,
or online at: www.kittiwake-books.com
See detailed descriptions at www.davidberrywalks.co.uk

Walks on the **Clwydian Range** – 22 walks

More Walks on the **Clwydian Range** – 23 walks

Walks in the **Vale of Clwyd** – 22 walks

Walks around **Llangollen & the Dee Valley** – 25 walks

Walks around **Holywell & Halkyn Mountain** – 20 walks

Walks in the **Hidden Heart of North Wales** – 21 walks

Walks around the **Berwyn Mountains & the Ceiriog Valley** – 32 walks

Walks around **Betws-y-Coed & the Conwy Valley** – 24 walks

Walks in the **Heart of Snowdonia** – 36 walks

Walks on the **Llŷn Peninsula** – 28 walks

Walks around **Y Bala & Penllyn** – 20 walks

Walks around **Barmouth & the Mawddach Estuary** – 20 walks

Walks around **Anglesey (Ynys Môn)** – 40 walks

Walks around **Conwy & the Foothills of Northern Snowdonia**– 30 walks

Walks around **Ruabon Mountain, The Clywedog Valley & Hope Mountain** – 28 walks

Walks around **Llandudno & along the coast to Prestatyn** – 30 walks

Walks around **Penmachno & Ysbyty Ifan** – 24 walks

Walks around **Chester & The Dee Estuary** – 26 walks

The Dee Way – 142 miles from source to sea

KITTIWAKE

Walks guides which detail superb routes
in most parts of Wales.

From Anglesey and Llandudno to the Brecon Beacons,
and from Machynlleth and Welshpool to Pembrokeshire and the Llŷn,
they offer a range of carefully researched routes
with something for all abilities.

Each guide has been compiled and written by a
dedicated author who really knows their particular area.

They are all presented in the **KITTIWAKE** clear
and easy-to-use style

For latest details of the expanding range, visit:

www.kittiwake-books.com

KITTIWAKE

3 Glantwymyn Village Workshops
Glantwymyn, Machynlleth
Montgomeryshire SY20 8LY